IBM®

PC APPRENTICE

PERSONAL COMPUTER LEARNING SERIES

UCSD Pascal® - beginning

Paul L. Schlieve, Ph.D.

Jon I. Young, Ph.D.

A PRENTICE-HALL/CHAMBERS TUTORIAL WORKBOOK

PRENTICE-HALL, INC., Englewood Cliffs, N.J. 07632

Coordinating Author/Instructional Design: **Russell A. Stultz**
Project Administrator: **Julia MacLauchlan**
Composition: **Dianne Stultz, Kay Dorsett**
Graphic Arts: **Alan McCuller**
Manufacturing: **Phillip Jowell**

This book is available at a special discount when ordered in bulk quantities. Contact Prentice-Hall, Inc., General Publishing Division, Special Sales, Englewood Cliffs, New Jersey 07632.

Printed in USA

10 9 8 7 6 5 4 3 2 1

ISBN 0-13-452400-4 Student Workbook
ISBN 0-13-452418-7 Course Administrator's Guide
ISBN 0-13-452988-X Self-teach Edition

Prentice-Hall International, Inc., *London*
Prentice-Hall of Australia Pty. Limited, *Sydney*
Prentice-Hall Canada, Inc., *Toronto*
Prentice-Hall of India Private Limited, *New Delhi*
Prentice-Hall of Japan, Inc., *Tokyo*
Prentice-Hall of Southeast Asia Pte. Ltd., *Singapore*
Whitehall Books Limited, Wellington, *New Zealand*
Editora Prentice-Hall do Brasil Ltda., *Rio de Janeiro*

STUDENT INFORMATION:

You will either receive a copy of the subject software from your teacher, school, bookstore, or learning center, in return for the properly completed Student Registration Card attached hereto or you will find the subject software contained in this package.

If you have received the software as a part of this package, you must complete and mail the Student Registration Card to the address shown on the card.

If the subject software does not accompany this workbook, you are probably enrolled in a program of study in which the IBM PC Apprentice Series is used and will be receiving the subject software from your educational institution. You will exchange the completed software.

DISKETTE LABEL(S)

Enclosed in this workbook are labels for use with the subject software. If you are receiving a copy of the software from your educational institution, you must immediately affix the label(s) to the diskette(s).

TEACHER INFORMATION:

The registration card provided below contains information about each student for your records. Once the cards are prepared by each student, you are authorized pursuant to the terms and conditions of the license contained in the Teacher Pack, to exchange one copy of the subject software (Educational Version) upon presentation of each completed Student Registration Card.

When you have collected the completed Student Registration Cards you must send them to the address on the back of the card.

SOFTWARE LICENSING

The software program(s) contained on the Educational Version diskette(s) has been generously provided by the copyright owner and is used with their permission in accordance with the terms and conditions of the enclosed license agreement. Unauthorized duplication of the diskette(s) is a violation of trust and law.

STUDENT REGISTRATION CARD

Please print when completing appropriate information.

Software Title ______________________ Course Title ______________________

Student Name ______________________

Home Address ______________________

City, State, Zip ______________________

Grade Level ________ Today's Date ______________________

Instructor's Name ______________________

School Name ______________________

Address ______________________

City, State, Zip ______________________

Computer Model (School) ______________________ (Home) ______________________

Place
Stamp
Here

Student Registration Office
4500 4th Street North
St. Petersburg, Florida 33703

SAMPLE EDUCATION INSTITUTION LICENSE AGREEMENT

SofTech Microsystems, Inc.
Apprentice Program License Agreement
(Apprentice Version Software)

YOU SHOULD CAREFULLY READ THE FOLLOWING TERMS AND CONDITIONS BEFORE OPENING THIS DISKETTE PACKAGE. OPENING THIS DISKETTE PACKAGE INDICATES YOUR ACCEPTANCE OF THESE TERMS AND CONDITIONS. IF YOU DO NOT AGREE WITH THEM, YOU SHOULD PROMPTLY RETURN THE PACKAGE UNOPENED, AND YOUR MONEY WILL BE REFUNDED.

"SofTech Microsystems, Inc. provides this program and licenses its use for educational purposes only. You assume responsibility for the selection of the program to achieve your intended results, and for the installation, use, and results obtained from the program. This license extends only to use of the program in the United States or countries in which the program is marketed by duly authorized distributors."

LICENSE

You may:

a. use the program on a single machine;

b. copy the program into any machine readable or printed form for backup purposes in support of your use of the program in accordance with this Agreement (Certain programs, however, may include mechanisms to limit or inhibit copying. They may be marked "copy protected.");

c. make and/or provide one copy of this program for educational purposes to each student who has purchased or been issued a new Prentice-Hall/Chambers Tutorial Workbook designed for use in conjunction with this program; provided, however, this program shall only be provided to each such student while enrolled in a course of study utilizing the program and related Prentice-Hall/ Chambers Tutorial Workbook; and

d. modify the program and/or merge it into another program in support of your use of the program in accordance with this Agreement (Any portion of this program merged into another program will continue to be subject to the terms and conditions of this Agreement.).

You must affix the SofTech Microsystems Apprentice Program License Abstract label and copyright notice provided with each Prentice-Hall/Chambers Tutorial Workbook to each copy of this program made hereunder.

YOU MAY NOT USE, COPY, MODIFY, OR TRANSFER THE PROGRAM, OR ANY COPY, MODIFICATION, OR MERGED PORTION, IN WHOLE OR IN PART, EXCEPT AS EXPRESSLY PROVIDED FOR IN THIS LICENSE.

EXCEPT AS EXPRESSLY PROVIDED FOR IN THIS LICENSE, IF YOU TRANSFER POSSESSION OF ANY COPY, MODIFICATION, OR MERGED PORTION OF THE PROGRAM TO ANOTHER PARTY, YOUR LICENSE IS AUTOMATICALLY TERMINATED.

TERM:

This license is effective for one year from the date this package is opened by you. You may terminate it at any other time by destroying the program, together with all copies, modifications, and merged portions in any form. It will also terminate upon conditions set forth elsewhere in this Agreement or if you fail to comply with any term or condition of this Agreement. You agree upon such termination to destroy the program together with all copies, modifications and merged portions in any form.

LIMITED WARRANTY

THE PROGRAM IS PROVIDED "AS IS" WITHOUT WARRANTY OF ANY KIND, EITHER EXPRESSED OR IMPLIED, INCLUDING, BUT NOT LIMITED TO THE IMPLIED WARRANTIES OF MERCHANTABILITY AND FITNESS FOR A PARTICULAR PURPOSE. THE ENTIRE RISK AS TO THE QUALITY AND PERFORMANCE OF THE PROGRAM IS WITH YOU. SHOULD THE PROGRAM PROVE DEFECTIVE, YOU (AND NOT SOFTECH MICROSYSTEMS OR ANY AUTHORIZED DISTRIBUTOR) ASSUME THE ENTIRE COST OF ALL NECESSARY SERVICING, REPAIR OR CORRECTION.

SOME STATES DO NOT ALLOW THE EXCLUSION OF IMPLIED WARRANTIES, SO THE ABOVE EXCLUSION MAY NOT APPLY TO YOU. THIS WARRANTY GIVES YOU SPECIFIC LEGAL RIGHTS AND YOU MAY ALSO HAVE OTHER RIGHTS WHICH VARY FROM STATE TO STATE.

SofTech Microsystems and the copyright owners do not warrant that the functions contained in the program will meet your requirements or that the operation of the program will be uninterrupted or error free.

However, SofTech Microsystems, through its authorized distributor, warrants the diskette(s) or cassettes on which the program is furnished, to be free from defects in materials and workmanship under normal use for a period of ninety (90) days from the date of delivery to you as evidenced by a copy of your receipt.

LIMITATIONS OF REMEDIES

SofTech Microsystems' and their authorized distributor's entire liability and your exclusive remedy shall be:

1. the replacement of any diskette or cassette not meeting SofTech Microsystems' "Limited Warranty" and which is returned to SofTech Microsystems or its authorized distributor with a copy of your purchase order, or

2. if SofTech Microsystems or the authorized distributor is unable to deliver a replacement diskette or cassette which is free of defects in materials or workmanship, you may terminate this Agreement by returning the program and your money will be refunded.

IN NO EVENT WILL SOFTECH MICROSYSTEMS, ANY COPYRIGHT OWNER OR ITS AUTHORIZED DISTRIBUTOR BE LIABLE TO YOU FOR ANY DAMAGES, INCLUDING ANY LOST PROFITS, LOST SAVINGS OR OTHER INCIDENTAL OR CONSEQUENTIAL DAMAGES ARISING OUT OF THE USE OR INABILITY TO USE SUCH PROGRAM EVEN IF SOFTECH MICROSYSTEMS OR AN AUTHORIZED DISTRIBUTOR HAS BEEN ADVISED OF THE POSSIBILITY OF SUCH DAMAGES, OR FOR ANY CLAIM BY ANY OTHER PARTY.

SOME STATES DO NOT ALLOW THE LIMITATION OR EXCLUSION OF LIABILITY FOR INCIDENTAL OR CONSEQUENTIAL DAMAGES SO THE ABOVE LIMITATION OR EXCLUSION MAY NOT APPLY TO YOU.

GENERAL

You may not sublicense, assign or transfer the license or the program except as expressly provided in this Agreement. Any attempt otherwise to sublicense, assign or transfer any of the rights, duties or obligations hereunder is void.

This Agreement will be governed by the laws of the State of California.

Should you have any questions concerning this Agreement, you may contact Prentice-Hall, Inc. by writing to:

Prentice-Hall, Inc.
General Publishing Division
Englewood Cliffs, NJ 07632

YOU ACKNOWLEDGE THAT YOU HAVE READ THIS AGREEMENT, UNDERSTAND IT AND AGREE TO BE BOUND BY ITS TERMS AND CONDITIONS. YOU FURTHER AGREE THAT IT IS THE COMPLETE AND EXCLUSIVE STATEMENT OF THE AGREEMENT BETWEEN US WHICH SUPERSEDES ANY PROPOSAL OR PRIOR AGREEMENT, ORAL OR WRITTEN, AND ANY OTHER COMMUNICATIONS BETWEEN US RELATING TO THE SUBJECT MATTER OF THIS AGREEMENT.

Contents

Part 9—Assignment Statement

Part 10—Character Variables and Type Matching

Part 11—Arithmetic and Numeric Output

Part 12—Input Statements

Part 13—Branching Statements

Part 14—For Loops

Part 15—Repeat And While Loops

PREFACE

WHAT IS THE P-SYSTEM?

The disk operating system of a computer is a software system which provides the means for the computer user to communicate with the computer, and for the computer to communicate with devices attached to it, such as the disk drives, display and printer. Traditional disk operating systems have been closely tied to a specific computer processor. As a result, translating programs from one computer to another has been a long and laborious undertaking.

The p-System addresses the issue of portability of computer programs from one computer to another by defining standard ways for computer programs to communicate with the keyboard, disk, screen and other devices.

WHAT IS PASCAL?

The fundamental machine language of computers, expressed as long strings of ones and zeros, is not easily understood by humans. In fact, understanding the function of more than very short segments of this code is almost impossible. As a result, there have been hundreds of attempts at designing a computer language which would allow more effectively designed programs to control computers. In this development process, some language features were discovered which make it easier to write structured, changeable computer code.

In 1968 Nicklaus Wirth designed the Pascal computer language for the purpose of teaching good programming practices to his students. Features of Pascal make it easy to express computer solutions to problems, and in some cases even make it difficult to write code which is likely to be confusing to the programmer. Pascal has evolved into a powerful and versatile language which is well suited for commercial software development as well as for its original purpose of teaching good programming habits.

ORGANIZATION

Learning about computer programming should be fun. That means you should learn about programming while using a computer. This workbook is designed to let you learn to use the p-System operating system and the Pascal computer language while actually working at the computer. The workbook contains fifteen *parts* that let you experiment with your computer and software as you learn.

PARTS The 15 *parts*, which are made up of *modules*, are intended to cover single learning sessions. However, parts may be divided or combined as needed to fit your schedule.

At the beginning of each part, you'll see a "What You Will Learn" heading and a list of learning goals. Reviewing this list shows you what the part has in store for you.

MODULES The modules in each part break topics down into small, easy-to-digest pieces. At the beginning of each module, a list of main topics, called *Key Topics*, is provided. This tells you what to watch for as you work your way through the module.

"Practice Sessions" let you use UCSD Pascal to develop and run computer programs. As you experiment with various program features, you find yourself learning by doing. This is the best way to learn new material. Clear, step-by-step instructions guide you through the programming process. Each session includes many illustrations showing computer screens. These let you check to see if you have followed the instructions.

The end of each module contains a Review. The Review lets you verify your new skills. If you are able to answer the review questions correctly, you are ready to go to the next module.

WHAT YOU SHOULD KNOW

Do not worry if you have never used a microcomputer. This course teaches microcomputer use from the ground up. Modules 1 through 4 introduce you to your microcomputer and UCSD Pascal.

In addition to learning about microcomputer operation and programming in UCSD Pascal, you will learn many new words and their meanings.

Welcome to the exciting world of microcomputers and UCSD Pascal. Have fun!

PART 1
GETTING STARTED

WHAT YOU WILL LEARN

- Equipment description
- Equipment connection
- Diskette handling and care
- Loading the system disk
- Starting the system

Module 1
SETTING UP

KEY TOPICS

- Equipment description
- Equipment connection
- Diskette handling and care
- Loading the system disk
- Starting the system

PRACTICE SESSION

Correct equipment handling procedures are critical if you are to get the best service from your computer system and its programs.

PREPARATION You need this workbook, the computer system unit, display monitor, and the IBM PC APPRENTICE diskette for UCSD Pascal.

LEARNING ACTIVITY Be sure to carefully read and follow these instructions and you won't have any problem learning about the equipment.

Equipment Description You may use one of several IBM microcomputers. All microcomputers have the same basic elements, which include:

1. Keyboard — Enters instructions and information.
2. Display monitor — Displays information.
3. Main chassis — Houses the following:
   - Central processing unit — Controls information flow and performs arithmetic operations.
   - Mass storage device(s) — Stores information on magnetic media (usually diskette drives).
   - Memory — Temporarily stores instructions and information.
   - Input-output circuits and connectors — Allow attachment of printers, telephone modems, and other computer devices.
   - Power supply — Provides electrical power to all circuits within the main chassis.

A simplified diagram of a microcomputer similar to the one you are using is contained in Figure 1-1.

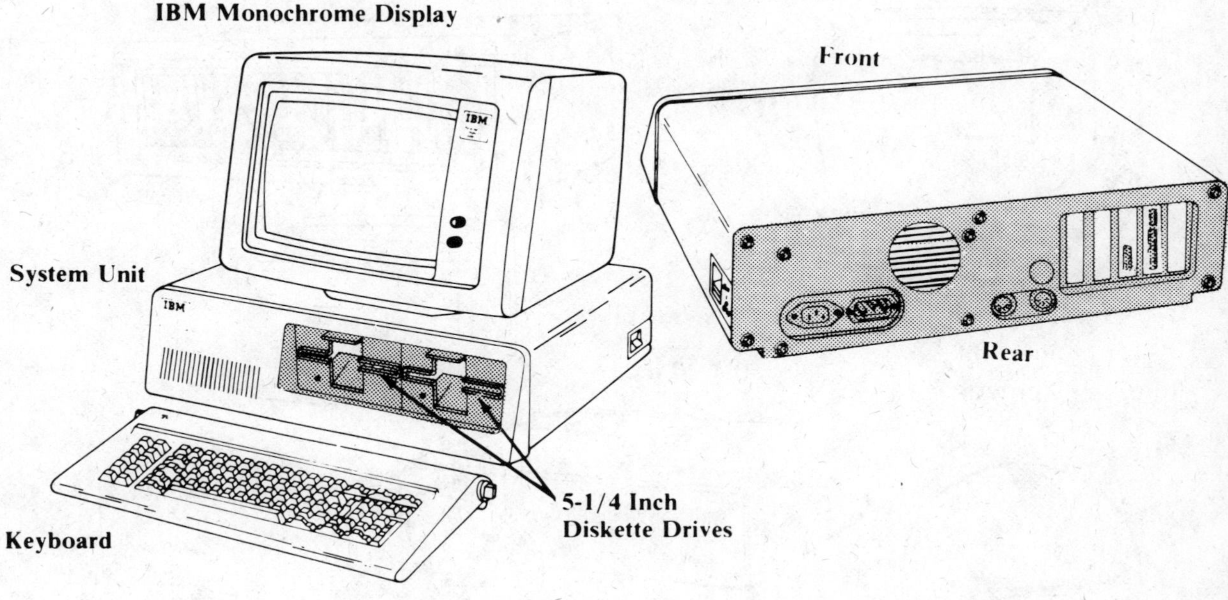

Figure 1-1 A typical microcomputer, simplified diagram

Equipment Connection. Before attempting to use your microcomputer for the first time, be sure it is properly connected and ready for use. Check the following connections. (See Figure 1-2)

- □ Display monitor cable is securely attached to the main chassis.
- □ Keyboard cable (for IBM PC, PC XT, and Portable PC) is connected between the keyboard and main chassis.
- □ Power switch is set to the OFF position. (Refer to figure 1-4.)
- □ Power cord is connected between main chassis and 115 vac wall outlet.
- □ Display monitor power cord is connected from the display unit to then and 115 VAC receptacle at the rear of the main chassis (IBM Monochrome Display only) or to a 115 VAC wall outlet.

If all cables and power cords are properly connected, check to see that the diskette drive or drives are empty and the load levers are open.

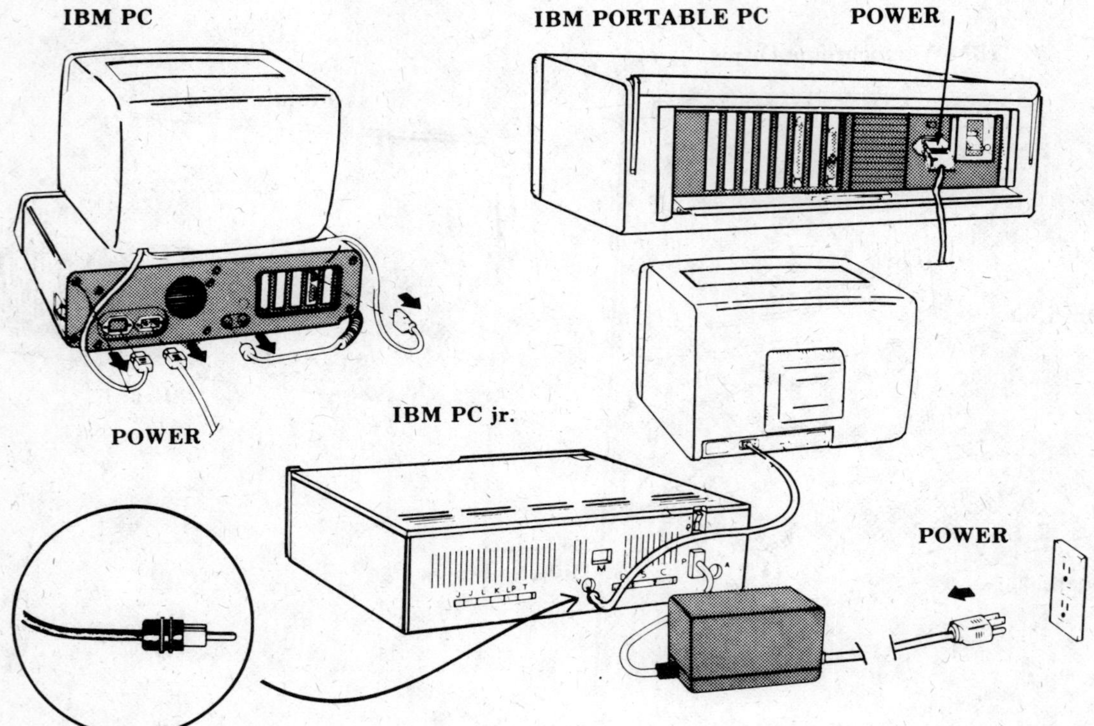

Figure 1-2 Equipment Connection Diagram

Diskette Handling and Storage Diskettes are delicate and should be handled accordingly.

1. Never touch the exposed surfaces; always hold diskettes by their paper jacket.

2. Never expose diskettes to
   a. Magnetic fields (Magnets, motors, heavy metal objects)
   b. Extreme heat or cold
   c. Moisture or oil
   d. Abrasive materials

3. Take care not to scratch, score, or prick the diskette or its protective cover.

4. Use a soft felt-tip marker when writing on diskette labels. Write lightly and avoid using ball-point or nylon-tip pens.

5. Store diskettes flat in a diskette case or box to avoid bending or folding.

Following these simple suggestions minimizes the possibility of damage to your valuable programs and stored information.

Loading the p-System Disk Operating System Now that everything is connected, you are ready to load a diskette. Find the diskette called "STUDENT:." This disk contains the disk operating system for this course. Look at Figure 1-3 while you follow the instructions.

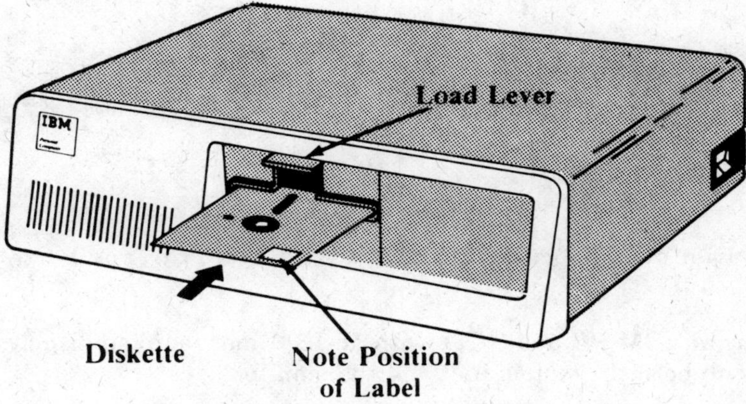

Figure 1-3 Inserting diskette into disk drive

1. Gently insert the STUDENT: diskette into the disk drive. If your computer has two disk drives, insert the disk in the drive on the left.

2. Close the load lever carefully. If it does not close, it means the diskette is not correctly inserted in the disk drive.

Starting the System The exact procedure you follow depends on which IBM computer you are working with.

1. Locate the power switch on the system unit. Refer to Figure 1-4 for the location of this switch on your system.

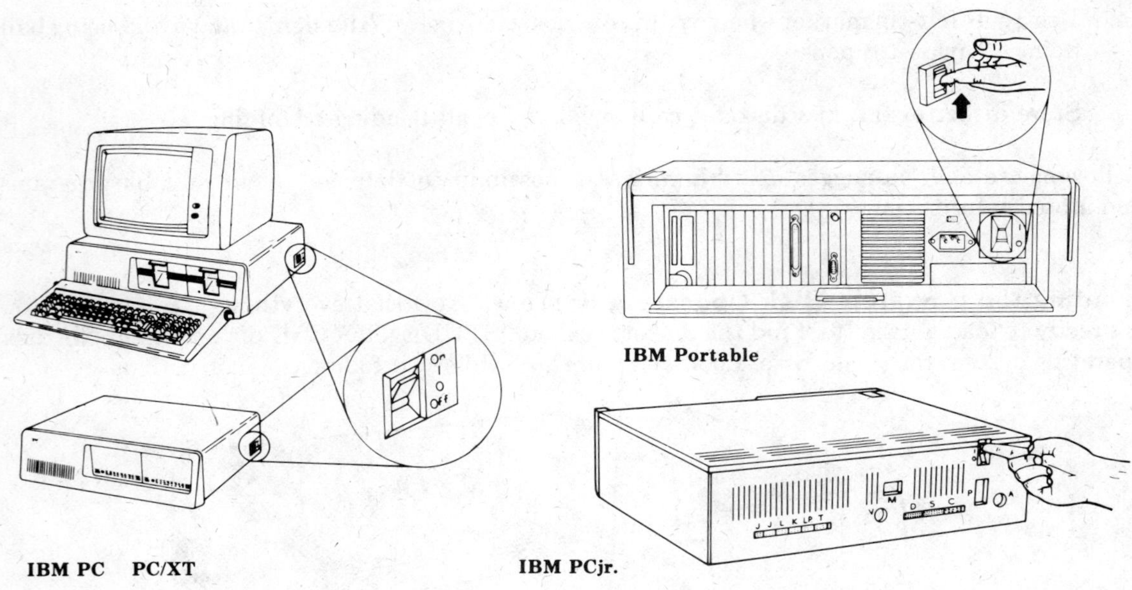

Figure 1-4 Power switch location for IBM PC, PC/XT, PCjr, and Portable

If you are using an IBM PC or PC/XT with an IBM monochrome display, this single switch provides power to both the system unit and the monitor.

If you are using an IBM Portable PC, the single power switch controls the power to all system elements.

If you are using an IBM PCjr, the system power switch and the monitor power switch must be turned on separately.

If you are using the IBM Color Display, locate the monitor power switch on the front panel of the monitor. Rotating this switch to the right turns it on.

2. Turn on your system unit and, if necessary, the monitor. It makes no difference which unit is turned on first.

NOTE

If you have a printer attached to your system, it needs to be turned on separately. It is not necessary to have the printer turned on yet, so let's save some energy and leave it off for now.

A computer in the IBM PC family has special circuits which give it a hardware checkup each time the computer is turned on. This process checks the internal workings of the computer prior to starting up. The length of time required to perform this check depends on the amount of memory installed in your computer. If your computer has a great deal of memory installed, this process takes about 90 seconds.

When the computer has finished its self-test it beeps, the light on the disk drive comes on, and you hear the disk drive spin while the computer transfers the p-System operating system information from the disk into the computer.

After about 30 seconds, the disk drive comes to a stop, and the computer will display the screen below welcoming you to the p-System.

WELCOME TO THE WORLD OF

UCSD PASCAL™

UCSD PASCAL™

UCSD PASCAL™

PRESENTED BY

SOFTECH™

MICROSYSTEMS

Press any key to continue

If you are using an IBM Monochrome Display your screen display is slightly different. If your screen doesn't display a UCSD Pascal logo, turn the main chassis off, make sure the diskette is the STUDENT:, that it is inserted correctly, and that the door to the disk drive is closed completely. Now turn the main chassis on again. If you still haven't the appropriate screen display, then seek assistance.

WHAT YOU HAVE LEARNED

- Recognize the parts of the computer system
- Connect the equipment

- Care for diskettes
- Insert the system diskette
- Turn on the system

REVIEW

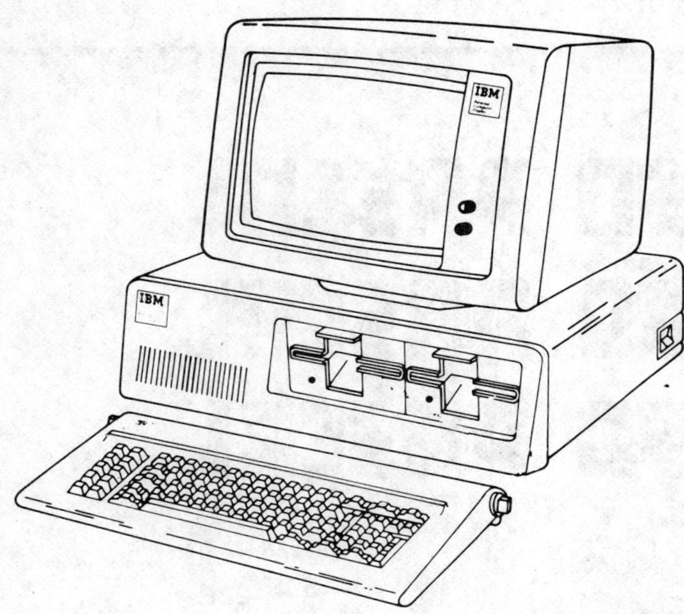

1. Label each component in the equipment diagram above with its name.

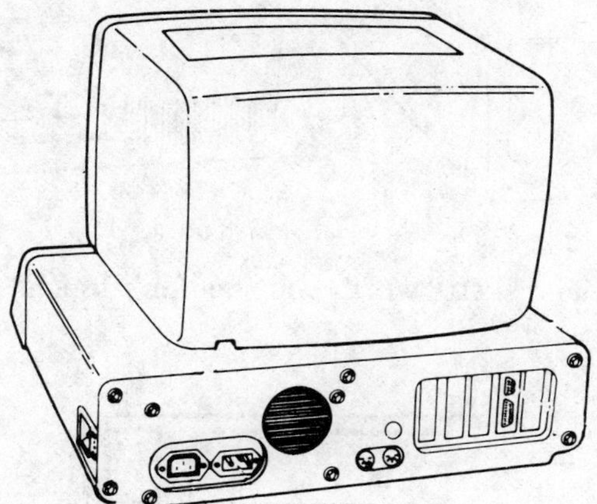

2. Draw and label the following cables in the figure:

   a. Display monitor cable
   b. Display monitor power cable
   c. Keyboard cable
   d. System unit power cable

3. List four ways a diskette can be damaged.

   a.
   b.
   c.
   d.

4. What is the name of the disk operating system you are using?

5. Which of the following diskettes is correctly positioned to be inserted in the disk drive?

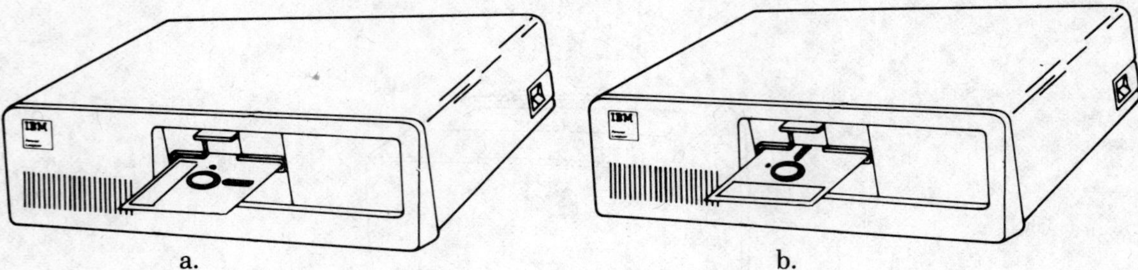

a.   b.

6. Blacken the areas of the diskette which you shouldn't touch.

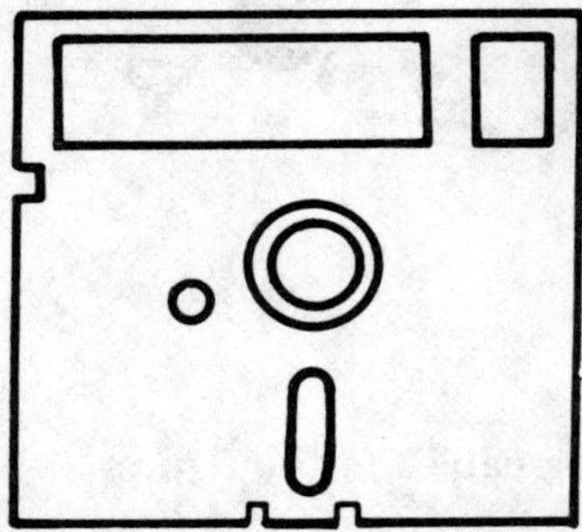

7. Name four things a diskette should not be exposed to.

a.
b.
c.
d.

8. Which action should you perform first when starting the system?

a. Turn on the power
b. Insert the diskette in the disk drive

PART 2
TOURING THE SYSTEM

WHAT YOU WILL LEARN

- Setting the system date
- Checking the volumes
- Listing files on a diskette
- Accessing SYSTEM.WRK.TEXT
- Inserting information
- Deleting insertions
- Compiler information
- Run
- Turn off computer

Module 2
TOURING THE FILER

KEY TOPICS

- Setting the system date
- Checking the volumes
- Listing files on a diskette

PRACTICE SESSION

Now that you have learned how to connect the parts of the computer system and how to start the p-System you are ready to learn how to use the features of the p-System. The first part of the p-System to explore is the Filer.

PREPARATION You already know how to connect the equipment and start the p-System software, so if you haven't already done so, do so now. Don't forget to insert the diskette before turning on the power.

1. Insert the p-System diskette and close the load lever.

2. Turn on power to the system unit and, if necessary, the monitor.

LEARNING ACTIVITY Now that the system is running, your screen display should look like the the one following.

```
Type <space> to continue
STUDENT:
SYSTEM.KEY           1 27-Apr-84     6   512  Datafile
SYSTEM.PASCAL      102 26-Apr-84     7   512  Datafile
SYSTEM.IBM.86       24 14-Feb-84   109   512  Datafile
SYSTEM.CONFIG       17  2-Sep-84   133   512  Datafile
SYSTEM.MISCINFO      1  2-Apr-84   150   226  Datafile
SYSTEM.FONT          2  4-Jan-84   151   512  Datafile
SYSTEM.FILER        39 26-Mar-84   153   512  Codefile
SYSTEM.EDITOR       51 26-Mar-84   192   512  Codefile
PRINT.CODE          17 14-Dec-82   243   512  Codefile
CONFIGURE.CODE      13 10-May-84   260   512  Codefile
LOGO.FONT            2 25-Apr-84   273   512  Datafile
DISKFORMAT.CODE     10 10-May-84   275   512  Codefile
SHOWDEMO.CODE        6 10-May-84   285   512  Codefile
SCRIPT.TEXT         42 10-May-84   291   512  Textfile
DEMO.TEXT            8 10-May-84   333   512  Textfile
DEMO.CODE            2 10-May-84   341   512  Codefile
SYSTEM.COMPILER    107 29-Mar-84   343   512  Codefile
SYSTEM.SYNTAX       14  4-May-83   450   512  Codefile
SYSTEM.LIBRARY      41  9-Apr-84   464   512  Copefile
SYSTEM.STARTUP      12 10-May-84   505   512  Codefile
SYSTEM.WRK.TEXT      4  2-Sep-86   517   512  Textfile
SYSTEM.WRK.CODE      2  2-Sep-86   521   512  Codefile
CANDO.TEXT           4  2-Sep-86   523   512  Textfile
```

1. Press the **Spacebar**.

The computer responds

```
Command: E(dit, R(un, F(ile, C(omp, X(ecute, U(ser restart [ED 1R0.0]
```

The Command Line The screen currently shown is the main command line. This screen indicates the major command groups of the p-System. You move from one group of commands to another through this screen. It is like the hub of a wheel, and the options displayed are the spokes on that wheel. To get from one spoke to another it is necessary to go through the hub.

Entering the Filer The command line lists several commands, followed by a cursor or "–". One of the options on the command line is the F(iler.

1. Type **F** to start the Filer.

The disk spins as the Filer program is loaded into the computer's memory. When the Filer is loaded, the Filer displays its own command line:

```
Filer: G(et, S(ave, W(hat, N(ew, L(dir, R(em, C(hng, T(rans, D(ate,? [ED 1.R0.0]
```

NOTE

The "?" near the end of the command line indicates that there are more commands available in the Filer than meet the eye.

2. Type **?** to see another screen of Filer commands.

The computer responds with:

```
Filer: Q(uit, B(ad-blks, E(xt-dir, K(rnch, M(ake, P(refix, V(ols, ? [ED 1R0.0]
```

This shows a second screen of Filer commands and another question mark at the end, indicating yet another screen of commands.

3. Type **?** to see the third screen of Filer commands.

The computer responds with:

```
Filer: X(amine, Z(ero, O(n/off-line, F(lip-swap/lock [ED 1R0.0]
```

This shows us the third (and final) screen of Filer commands. There is no question mark at the end of the line. That doesn't mean that typing it won't work; it simply returns you to the primary Filer screen.

4. Type **?** to return to the first screen of Filer commands.

The computer responds:

```
Filer: G(et, S(ave, W(hat, N(ew, L(dir, R(em, C(hng, T(rans, D(ate,? [ED 1.R0.0]
```

Setting the Date Setting the date is a function of the Filer.

1. Type **D** for D(ate. Notice the following display.

```
Date set: <1..31>-<Jan..Dec>-<00..99>
 Today is 22-Mar-84
 New date ?
```

The "Today is" date shown on the screen is the date entered the last time the date was set. The p-System uses this date to help you keep track of the last time you made changes to your programs and data. Since it is not 22-Mar-84, you need to tell the computer the correct date.

Type in today's date using the pattern shown. If you make a mistake while typing, use the **Backspace** key to correct your typing errors.

2. Type the day of the month first, then type –.

3. Type the first three letters of the current month, then type –. Use either upper- or lowercase letters.

4. Type the last two digits of the current year.

5. Press the **Enter** key and check your new date for accuracy. The **Enter** key looks like this ◄┘ and is found near the right side of the keyboard.

6. Type **D**.

Your new date is now the current date. This date remains in effect until you change it. If your new date is not correct, change it now by typing the correct date. If the current date is correct, simply press **Enter** without making any changes.

It is not necessary to type all three parts of the date (date-month-year) every day. It is only necessary to type the parts of the date that have changed. For example, if we type **D** for the Date and get the screen below

```
Date set: <1..31>-<Jan..Dec>-<00-99>
 Today is 21-Sep-87
 New date ?
```

and the date is really the 22nd of September, it is only necessary to type the date; the month and year need not be typed again until they change. To change the date from September 21, 1987, to September 22, 1987, you only need to type **22** in response to the new date prompt and then press **Enter**.

Checking the Volumes The p-System refers to all of the elements of your microcomputer system as volumes. The V(olume command from the F(iler screen allows you to examine a list of the volumes currently attached to the system. Your screen should show the Filer command line at the top.

```
Filer: G(et, S(ave, W(hat, N(ew, L(dir, R(em, C(hng, T(rans, D(ate,? [ED 1.R0.0]
```

A quick inspection of the command line reveals that there is no V(olume command displayed. The V(olume command is on the second screen of Filer commands.

1. Type **?**.

```
Filer: Q(uit, B(ad-blks, E(xt-dir, K(rnch, M(ake, P(refix, V(ols, ? [ED 1R0.0]
```

The display you now see shows the second screen of Filer commands. It is not necessary to have the command showing in order to use it, but it is a helpful reminder. Notice that this screen of commands contains the "V(ols" command.

2. Type **V** for V(olume. Notice the following display. Your display may be slightly different from the one shown, as the p-System automatically adjusts itself according to the optional equipment installed in your computer.

```
Filer: G(et, S(ave, W(hat, N(ew, L(dir, R(em, C(hng, T(rans, D(ate,? [ED 1.R0.0]
 Vols on-line:
   1    CONSOLE:
   2    SYSTERM:
   4 #  STUDENT: [  720]
   6    PRINTER:
Root vol is - STUDENT:
Prefix is   - STUDENT:
```

The p-System has assigned the elements of your computer to numbered volumes as follows:

1. CONSOLE: This is the display monitor.

2. SYSTERM: This is the keyboard.

(3. Although there is space here for another piece of hardware, it may not be used in your microcomputer.)

4. Disk Drive: Notice that the name of this volume is STUDENT:. The p-System allows you to give each disk its own name. The number (720) following the name of the diskette refers to the storage capacity of the diskette.

(5. This space is reserved for a second disk drive. The IBM PC APPRENTICE version of the p-System recognizes only one disk drive, so this space is not assigned in your system.)

6. PRINTER: Your microcomputer has provisions for a printer.

7. REMIN: This is where another computer would send messages to your computer. This option may not be installed in your computer.

8. REMOUT: This is where your computer would send information to another computer. This option may not be installed in your computer.

(9-99. These numbers are reserved for other equipment which may be part of your computer system. This equipment might be real physical equipment, like an additional disk drive, or it might be virtual (simulated) equipment, such as the assignment of extra memory in your computer as an electronic RAMDISK:. Devices 9-99 are not supported by the IBM PC APPRENTICE version of the p-System.)

The "Root" volume and "Prefix" volume notations at the bottom of the screen are primarily used with multiple disk drive systems.

Listing Files Now you are ready to list the names of all the files of information on the disk drive in your microcomputer. Notice that the V(olume command placed the list of volumes on the screen, then immediately placed the Filer command line back at the top of the screen, ready for another Filer command.

At the top of your screen, locate the L(Dir option. This option causes a list of the file directory to be displayed on the screen.

1. Type **L**.

Your computer accepts this command but needs more information to carry out the process. It asks for this information on the screen:

```
Dir listing of what vol?
```

Now the computer wants to know which volume you want to examine. Looking at the list of volumes, which is still on the screen from the last operation, you can see that only one of the volumes on the system has files to list. That volume is the diskette in unit #4 named "STUDENT:".

There are three ways to reference this diskette.

a. You can type it's name, **STUDENT:**.

b. You can type the number of the disk drive, **#4:**. If you use the number of the disk drive, the system does not check for the name of the diskette.

c. You can take advantage of the fact that STUDENT: is the "root" volume. You can refer to the root volume by typing *.

2. Type **STUDENT:**. The colon is important, don't forget it.

NOTE
Typing * or **#4:** would mean the same thing in this case.

3. Press **Enter**.

Your display monitor provides you a display which looks like this:

```
Filer: G(et, S(ave, W(hat, N(ew, L(dir, R(em, C(hng, T(rans, D(ate,? [ED 1.R0.0]
STUDENT:
SYSTEM.KEY          1 27-Apr-84
SYSTEM.PASCAL     102 26-Apr-84
SYSTEM.IBM.86      24 14-Feb-84
SYSTEM.CONFIG      17  2-Sep-84
SYSTEM.MISCINFO     1  2-Apr-84
SYSTEM.FONT         2  4-Jan-84
SYSTEM.FILER       39 26-Mar-84
SYSTEM.EDITOR      51 26-Mar-84
PRINT.CODE         17 14-Dec-82
CONFIGURE.CODE     13 10-May-84
LOGO.FONT           2 25-Apr-84
DISKFORMAT.CODE    10 10-May-84
```

```
SHOWDEMO.CODE      6 10-May-84
SCRIPT.TEXT       42 10-May-84
DEMO.TEXT          8 10-May-84
DEMO.CODE          2 10-May-84
SYSTEM.COMPILER  107 29-Mar-84
SYSTEM.SYNTAX     14  4-May-83
SYSTEM.LIBRARY    41  9-Apr-84
SYSTEM.STARTUP    12 10-May-84
20/20 files<listed/in-dir>, 517 blocks used, 203 unused, 203 in largest
```

NOTE

There may be some minor variations between the listing above and your screen display as UCSD Pascal and the p-System are subject to periodic improvements. If minor variations in file sizes or dates occur, there is no cause for concern.

The directory lists all of the files found on the diskette volume STUDENT:. The display shows each file's name and the date it was created or last changed.

The last line of your display indicates that there are 20 files on the diskette and 20 listed in the directory. You are also told that there are 203 blocks of storage available on the diskette.

This diskette has a total of 720 blocks of space available, 517 of which are taken by the p-System, the Pascal compiler, and utility programs.

Extended Directory There is another option provided to show additional information about the files on the diskette.

1. Type **E**.

```
Dir listing of what vol?
```

2. This time, type * for the "root volume."

The computer responds by displaying a new screen,

```
Filer: G(et, S(ave, W(hat, N(ew, L(dir, R(em, C(hng, T(rans, D(ate,? [ED 1.R0.0]
STUDENT:
SYSTEM.KEY          1 27-Apr-84     6   512  Datafile
SYSTEM.PASCAL     102 26-Apr-84     7   512  Datafile
SYSTEM.IBM.86      24 14-Feb-84   109   512  Datafile
SYSTEM.CONFIG      17  2-Sep-84   133   512  Datafile
SYSTEM.MISCINFO     1  2-Apr-84   150   226  Datafile
SYSTEM.FONT         2  4-Jan-84   151   512  Datafile
SYSTEM.FILER       39 26-Mar-84   153   512  Codefile
SYSTEM.EDITOR      51 26-Mar-84   192   512  Codefile
PRINT.CODE         17 14-Dec-82   243   512  Codefile
CONFIGURE.CODE     13 10-May-84   260   512  Codefile
LOGO.FONT           2 25-Apr-84   273   512  Datafile
DISKFORMAT.CODE    10 10-May-84   275   512  Codefile
SHOWDEMO.CODE       6 10-May-84   285   512  Codefile
SCRIPT.TEXT        42 10-May-84   291   512  Textfile
DEMO.TEXT           8 10-May-84   333   512  Textfile
DEMO.CODE           2 10-May-84   341   512  Codefile
SYSTEM.COMPILER   107 29-Mar-84   343   512  Codefile
SYSTEM.SYNTAX      14  4-May-83   450   512  Codefile
SYSTEM.LIBRARY     41  9-Apr-84   464   512  Copefile
SYSTEM.STARTUP     12 10-May-84   505   512  Codefile
< UNUSED >        203             517
20/20 files<listed/in-dir>, 517 blocks used, 203 unused, 203 in largest
```

E is the command for the extended directory, and this display provides additional information about each file. Your screen may have some minor variations in dates and file sizes as the p-System is continually improved, but the format of the display is the same.

The additional columns of information give you more information about the exact size and nature of each file. The first column of information contains the names of the files on the disk. The files are recorded on the disk in the order listed. All the unused space is grouped at the end of the disk.

The second column of information is the length of each file in blocks.

The third column is the date the file was created or last changed.

The fourth column is the starting block number for the file. The first file starts in block number 6 because the system reserves the first five blocks for its own use and doesn't share their contents with us.

The fifth column is the length of each block in bytes.

The sixth and last column designates the type of each file. There are three types of files on this disk: Datafile, Codefile, and Textfile. All of the blocks through 517 are full, and blocks 518 through 720 are empty.

Most users of the p-System routinely use the **E** Filer command instead of the **L** command when wanting to consult the diskette directory. The **E** command provides more information with no additional effort. The **L** command was included in the system for compatibility with other computers with much slower printing displays. When using a high speed video display, like the one you are using, it takes little additional time and no additional effort to display the extended directory instead of the short directory.

Quitting the Filer This concludes your brief visit to the Filer. It is now necessary to leave the Filer and return to the hub of the system, the main command line.

1. Type **?**.
2. Locate the Q(uit command on the command line.
3. Type **Q** to quit the Filer and return to the main command line.

Quitting the Filer returns you to the main command line, and your screen has the command line displayed at the top.

WHAT YOU HAVE LEARNED

- Set the system date
- List the volumes
- List the files on a diskette

REVIEW

1. To start the Filer you need to type what command?
2. What does the **?** command on the Filer command line allow you to do?
3. When the cursor appears on the screen at the end of the command line, what should you do?
4. Starting from the main command line, what command sequence calls up the date display?
5. Write the date as you would to enter in the computer for January 22, 1987.

6. Draw the symbol for the **Enter** key.

7. What command is typed to list the Volumes?

8. Define the following terms:

   a. SYSTERM:

   b. REMIN:

   c. CONSOLE:

   d. REMOUT:

9. What is necessary to view the "Root volume?"

10. What do you type to display the names and limited information about the diskette files?

11. How many total blocks of storage are available on your diskette?

12. What command displays a detailed listing of the files on the diskette, showing exactly which blocks of storage each file occupies?

Module 3
TOURING THE EDITOR

KEY TOPICS

- Accessing SYSTEM.WRK.TEXT
- Inserting information
- Deleting insertions

PRACTICE SESSION

The Editor is the primary means through which you interact with the computer system. The Editor allows you to create and modify files of computer program statements in the development of computer software.

PREPARATION In Module 2 you explored the Filer, one of the major software spokes which radiates from the hub of the main command screen. In this module you explore the Editor, a second major spoke from the central hub. To begin this practice session, make sure that you have the p-System loaded in your computer with the main command screen displayed.

LEARNING ACTIVITY Your display should show the main command line.

```
Command: E(dit, R(un, F(ile, C(omp, X(ecute, U(ser restart [ED 1R0.0]
```

Accessing SYSTEM.WRK.TEXT The p-System provides a file named SYSTEM.WRK.TEXT which it uses as a development file when you are writing and running programs. When you type the **E** command, the system needs to know whether you want to edit a specific file, or work with the system provided workfile.

1. Type **E** for the command E(ditor.

The screen displays the message:

```
>Edit
 No workfile is present. File? ( <ret> for no file  ) _
```

This display says that no workfile has been created. This is understandable since this is the first time you have used the Editor. For now, we let the system provide us with its built-in file. The screen tells you to press <ret> to let the system provide the file for you. On the IBM PC family, the **Enter** key provides the <ret> function.

2. Press **Enter**.

Now the computer is ready for you to type program statements into the working file SYSTEM.WRK.TEXT. Your display looks like this,

```
>Edit: A(djust C(opy D(el F(ind I(nsert J(ump K(ol M(argin P(age ? [ED 1R0.0]
```

This shows the first screen of commands available in the Editor. The question mark shows you that there are additional Editor commands available.

3. Type **?** to see the additional Editor commands.

The computer responds:

```
>Edit: Q(uit R(plc S(et V(erify X(ch Z(ap [ED 1R0.0]
```

The absence of a question mark tells you that this is the last screen of commands in the Editor.

4. Type **?** to return to the main Editor screen.

```
>Edit: A(djust C(opy D(el F(ind I(nsert J(ump K(ol M(argin P(age ? [ED 1R0.0]
```

NOTE

If you make a mistake while in the Editor and don't know how to recover, press the **Esc** key. This cancels whatever function you tried unsuccessfully to perform and returns you to the Editor command line.

Inserting Information Since we want to create a file with computer program statements, we need to be in the Insert mode.

1. Type **I** for I(nsert.

Your computer display now displays the I(nsert menu instead of the Filer menu.

```
>Insert: Text {<bs> a char, <del> a line} [<ext> accepts, <esc> escapes]
```

The Insert mode of the Editor allows you to type information into the computer to be stored in a TEXT file. The next step is to type a simple computer program into the computer and follow the process through the editing, compiling, and running of the program.

2. Type the following lines of text *exactly* as printed below. Double check that you have included all the required single quotation marks and semicolons. Press **Enter** after each line is finished.

```
PROGRAM FIRST;
BEGIN
      WRITE('I con do it!');
END.
```

This is a very simple program. Be sure to type it exactly as it appears here, including spelling the word "con" exactly as printed.

a. Did you indent the third line four spaces? Use the **spacebar** to do this.

b. Place the END statement directly under the BEGIN statement. You need to use the **backspace** key ◄— to do this.

c. Text can be typed in capital or lowercase characters. The computer doesn't care.

Delete Insertion If you make a mistake, you can erase or delete information. Use the **backspace** key until you have backed over the incorrect material. Then type the correct material.

1. Press **backspace** now until the cursor has backed over the letter "o" in "con."

2. Retype the correct character **a** and type the rest of the text.

Accepting Changes Now that you have correctly typed the text on the screen, you need to tell the Editor what to do with it. The procedure to accept this insertion is **Ctrl-C**. The **Ctrl** key has no meaning by itself. It can only change the meaning of other keys. To use the **Ctrl** key functions you must press and hold the **Ctrl** key while typing the other key.

1. Press and hold the **Ctrl**.

2. Type and release the **C** key while continuing to hold down the **Ctrl** key.

3. Release the **Ctrl** key.

The Editor has accepted your input and returned you to the Edit command line.

```
>Edit: A(djust C(opy D(el F(ind I(nsert J(ump K(ol M(argin P(age ? [ED 1R0.0]
```

Your program is now complete, and it is time to save it on the floppy disk. Quit the Editor.

4. Type **Q** for Quit.

The computer responds:

```
>Quit:
      U(pdate the workfile and leave
      E(xit without updating
      R(eturn to the editor without updating
      W(rite to a file name and return
```

There are four different ways to quit, and the Editor needs to know which one you want to use. For this module, use the **U** option to U)pdate the work file and leave.

5. Type **U** for U)pdate the workfile and leave.

The computer confirms your selection to save the file and displays:

```
Writing..
Your file is 58 bytes long.
```

When the write operation is complete, the command line reappears at the top of the screen.

```
Command: E(dit, R(un, F(ile, C(omp, X(ecute, U(ser restart [ED 1R0.0]
 Writing..
 Your file is 58 bytes long.
```

You are now out of the Editor and back at the central hub of the main command screen.

WHAT YOU HAVE LEARNED

- Start the Editor
- Access the file SYSTEM.WRK.TEXT
- Add new text with the Editor
- Delete text prior to acceptance
- Accept input text
- Quit the Editor
- Save the edited file on the diskette

REVIEW

1. What is the command to access the Editor?

2. The **Enter** key on your IBM computer performs the function of what key on other computers?

3. What is the symbol for the **Enter key**?

4. When typing text, you need to use which case, upper or lower?

5. To erase an unwanted character while in the Input mode you can use which key?

6. Which keys, when pressed at the same time, tell the computer that you are finished entering text?

7. What is the command to create a new file?

8. What key permits you to leave the Editor?

9. What is SYSTEM.WRK.TEXT?

10. What does the **Esc** key do when performing one of the Editor functions?

Module 4
COMPILE AND RUN

KEY TOPICS

- Compiler information
- Run
- Turn off computer

PRACTICE SESSION

In this module, you use the Pascal Compiler to translate the program you wrote and saved in the file SYSTEM.WRK.TEXT into code that the computer can understand. You then run the program and see the results of your efforts.

PREPARATION In Module 3 you used the Editor to create the program

```
PROGRAM FIRST;
BEGIN
  WRITE('I can do it!');
END.
```

and save it on the diskette in a file named SYSTEM.WRK.TEXT. Now that you have created a program, the next step is to get the computer to follow those instructions. The computer does not understand the program you wrote in its present form. All the computer understands are the ones and zeros of binary arithmetic. It is therefore necessary to translate the program you wrote into a code the computer can understand. In the p-System, this code is called p-code. Fortunately, this translation process is simple, because the p-System provides you with an automatic translator program called a compiler that performs this function for you.

If you are unsure about whether or not your program is there, enter the Filer from the main command line and use the L(Directory command to display your files on the screen. Look for the file SYSTEM.WRK.TEXT. It should be the last file on the list. Now Q(uit the Filer and return to the main command line. If SYSTEM.WRK.TEXT is not on the list, return to Module 3 and create this file.

LEARNING ACTIVITY Your display monitor should show the main command line now.

```
Command: E(dit, R(un, F(ile, C(omp, X(ecute, U(ser restart [ED 1R0.0]
```

Compiler Information One of the commands shown is the C(ompile command. At this command the translator starts to translate your Pascal text into p-code.

1. Type **C**.

There is a brief pause before the next screen appears while the computer loads the Compiler into memory and prepares to begin work on your program. When it is ready to begin, it displays

```
Compiling...
Output file for compiled listing? (<cr> for none)
```

2. Press **Enter**.

The Compiler begins its work. This program is extremely short, so the Compiler finishes rapidly. Notice that as it does its work, the Compiler places a series of dots on the screen. This is to let you know that it really is working and hasn't just gone away and forgotten about you. The screen display looks like this:

```
Compiling...
Output file for compiled listing?  (<cr> for none)

Pascal compiler - release level [ED 1R0.0]
<     0>..
FIRST
<     2>.

FIRST     .
```

The top line of your screen automatically returns to the command line.

```
Command: E(dit, R(un, F(ile, C(omp, X(ecute, U(ser restart [ED  1R0.0]
```

Run Your Pascal program has now been translated into p-code, a language that your computer (with the help of a p-code interpreter built into the p-System) can now use. Locate the R(un follow the instructions in your compiled Pascal program. In fact, the R(un command is quite smart. If you forget to compile your program, the R(un command does it for you automatically.

1. Type **R**.

The computer now transfers control to your program, and the display reads

```
Running...
I can do it!
```

When the computer has finished running your program, it once again takes control of the system, and places the command line back at the top of the screen.

```
Command: E(dit, R(un, F(ile, C(omp, X(ecute, U(ser restart [ED 1R0.0]
 Running...
 I can do it!
```

This whole process happened so quickly you may have missed it. If you did, try typing **R** again to repeat the process.

CAUTION

If you turn the computer off while the red light on the disk drive is lit, there is an excellent chance that you will lose your information and possibly make the entire disk unreadable. Never turn the computer off while the disk drive is in use.

WHAT YOU HAVE LEARNED

- Compile a program
- Run a program
- Turn off the computer

REVIEW

1. What is a simple definition of *compile*?

2. How do you know the disk drive is in operation?

3. What does the R(un command do?

4. What happens if you forget to C(ompile your program before using the R(un command?

5. Under what two conditions is it most appropriate to turn off the computer?

   a. ______________________________

   b. ______________________________

PART 3
USING THE FILER

WHAT YOU WILL LEARN

- Create filenames
- Change filenames
- Copy files to the screen
- Copy files on the diskette
- Copy files to the printer
- Erase files on the diskette
- Check diskette for damage
- Consolidate unused space on the diskette

Module 5
TRANSFERRING FILES

KEY TOPICS

- Create filenames
- Change filenames
- Copy files to the screen
- Copy files on the diskette
- Copy files to the printer
- Erase files on the diskette

PRACTICE SESSION

Since you have been introduced to the p-System, you are ready to examine each feature in greater detail. The first feature you must be able to use is the Filer.

PREPARATION If you have not already done so, start the computer by inserting the STUDENT: diskette in the disk drive and turning on the power. Use the Filer to set the system date. Quit the Filer and return to the command line.

Format a Blank Diskette You need a second diskette for this module which has been formatted for the p—System. There is a computer program on your STUDENT: diskette named DISKFORMAT.CODE. The function of this program is to prepare a blank diskette for use by the p-System.

1. Type **X** for X(ecute.

```
Execute what file? _
```

2. Type **DISKFORMAT** and press **Enter**.

```
Diskette format routine - revision [ED 1R1.1]
==================================================================================

Insert a blank, double-sided diskette into drive #4:

then hit any key to format the disk or "A" to abort formatting
```

3. Remove the STUDENT: diskette and insert a blank diskette in the drive.

4. Press a key other than **A**.

The following screen develops as the diskette is formatted:

```
Diskette format routine - revision [ED 1R1.1]
==================================================================================

Formatting side 0
........................................

Formatting side 1
........................................
```

When the diskette is successfully formatted, the screen displays:

```
Diskette format routine - revision [ED 1R1.1]
==================================================================================

720 block disk formatted.

Directory initialized to be "BLANK"

Type <space> to continue
```

5. Press the **Spacebar**.

```
Command: E(dit, R(un, F(ile, C(omp, X(ecute, U(ser restart [ED 1R0.0]
```

6. Remove the formatted diskette and replace it with STUDENT:.

The diskette you have formatted has the name BLANK:.

LEARNING ACTIVITY Transferring files is a function of the Filer.

1. Type **F** to start the Filer.

```
Filer: G(et, S(ave, W(hat, N(ew, L(dir, R(em, C(hng, T(rans, D(ate,? [ED 1R0.0]
```

2. Type **E*** and press **Enter** to list the extended directory on the screen.

```
Filer: G(et, S(ave, W(hat, N(ew, L(dir, R(em, C(hng, T(rans, D(ate,? [ED 1.R0.0]
STUDENT:
SYSTEM.KEY          1 27-Apr-84    6   512  Datafile
SYSTEM.PASCAL     102 26-Apr-84    7   512  Datafile
SYSTEM.IBM.86      24 14-Feb-84  109   512  Datafile
SYSTEM.CONFIG      17  2-Sep-84  133   512  Datafile
SYSTEM.MISCINFO     1  2-Apr-84  150   226  Datafile
SYSTEM.FONT         2  4-Jan-84  151   512  Datafile
SYSTEM.FILER       39 26-Mar-84  153   512  Codefile
SYSTEM.EDITOR      51 26-Mar-84  192   512  Codefile
PRINT.CODE         17 14-Dec-82  243   512  Codefile
CONFIGURE.CODE     13 10-May-84  260   512  Codefile
LOGO.FONT           2 25-Apr-84  273   512  Datafile
DISKFORMAT.CODE    10 10-May-84  275   512  Codefile
SHOWDEMO.CODE       6 10-May-84  285   512  Codefile
SCRIPT.TEXT        42 10-May-84  291   512  Textfile
DEMO.TEXT           8 10-May-84  333   512  Textfile
DEMO.CODE           2 10-May-84  341   512  Codefile
SYSTEM.COMPILER   107 29-Mar-84  343   512  Codefile
SYSTEM.SYNTAX      14  4-May-83  450   512  Codefile
SYSTEM.LIBRARY     41  9-Apr-84  464   512  Copefile
```

```
SYSTEM.STARTUP    12 10-May-84   505   512  Codefile
< UNUSED >           203             517
20/20 files<listed/in-dir>, 517 blocks used, 203 unused, 203 in
largest
```

The editing and compiling you did with the program to print "I can do it!" created two new files, SYSTEM.WRK.TEXT and SYSTEM.WRK.CODE, which prevent the entire directory from fitting on a single screen.

3. Press the **Spacebar** to see the remainder of the directory.

```
Filer: G(et, S(ave, W(hat, N(ew, L(dir, R(em, C(hng, T(rans, D(ate,? [ED 1R0.0]
STUDENT:
22/22 files<listed/in-dir>, 523 blocks used, 197 unused, 197 in largest
```

Describe Filenames The system does not allow you to name a file just anything, the name must obey certain rules.

a. The filename must be entirely composed of letters (A-Z), numerals (0-9), or the characters period (.), dash (—), underline (_), slash (/), or backslash(\).

b. The maximum length of a filename is 15 characters.

Certain filename endings have special meanings to the p-System. A file of text like the file SYSTEM.WRK.TEXT, which you used to write your program in Module 3, ends in ".TEXT" so that it can be used by the Editor. The Editor can only work on files ending in ".TEXT." The Pascal compiler refuses to compile a file which does not have a name ending in ".TEXT."

One of the commands available in the Filer is the M(ake command, which makes a file for you. This command does not place any information in the file; it just creates an empty file. You could think of this as placing a label on an empty file folder and placing the folder in the file cabinet.

1. Press the **Spacebar** to clear the screen.

2. Type **M** to M(ake a file.

Your screen displays:

```
Make what file ?
```

The system asks you to supply a filename. It also needs to know how large you want the file. If you don't tell the system the length of the file, it makes it as large as possible. The length is specified in blocks and is placed in square brackets immediately following the filename. Let's first try an unacceptable filename and give it a length of ten blocks.

3. Type **SCHOOL.BUDGET.1992.ATHLETICS.TEXT**

The computer may respond with an error message indicating that the maximum file length is 15 characters. Then again, it may simply ignore your request and return to the Filer command line. In either case, the system does not permit you to call a file by a name longer than 15 characters. As a result, your file has not been created.

Let's try to create a file which is larger than the space available on the diskette.

4. Type **M**.

The computer responds:

```
Make what file ?
```

5. Type **BUDGET87.TEXT(1000)** and press **Enter**.

The computer responds:

```
Filer: G(et, S(ave, W(hat, N(ew, L(dir, R(em, C(hng, T(rans, D(ate,? [ED 1R0.0]
No room on vol
```

Let's try breaking another rule, and use an invalid character, **$**.

6. Type **M**.

The computer responds:

```
Make what file ?
```

7. Type **BUDGET$87.TEXT(10)** and press **Enter**.

The screen displays:

```
Filer: G(et, S(ave, W(hat, N(ew, L(dir, R(em, C(hng, T(rans, D(ate,? [ED 1R0.0]
STUDENT:BUDGET87.TEXT made
```

You can see that the system does not let you call a file by a name that doesn't follow the rule of using only approved characters. The system helps you by ignoring the invalid character "$." Unlike the previous examples, this time the computer corrected your error and made the file for you. To verify that your file was actually created, call up the directory on the screen again.

8. Type **E**.

The computer responds:

```
Dir of what volume ?
```

9. Type **#4:** and press **Enter**.

The computer now displays your file BUDGET87.TEXT at the bottom of the list of files. The length of the file is shown as 10 blocks, just as you specified.

```
Type <space> to continue
STUDENT:
SYSTEM.KEY           1 27-Apr-84     6    512  Datafile
SYSTEM.PASCAL      102 26-Apr-84     7    512  Datafile
SYSTEM.IBM.86       24 14-Feb-84   109    512  Datafile
SYSTEM.CONFIG       17  2-Sep-84   133    512  Datafile
SYSTEM.MISCINFO      1  2-Apr-84   150    226  Datafile
SYSTEM.FONT          2  4-Jan-84   151    512  Datafile
SYSTEM.FILER        39 26-Mar-84   153    512  Codefile
SYSTEM.EDITOR       51 26-Mar-84   192    512  Codefile
PRINT.CODE          17 14-Dec-82   243    512  Codefile
CONFIGURE.CODE      13 10-May-84   260    512  Codefile
LOGO.FONT            2 25-Apr-84   273    512  Datafile
DISKFORMAT.CODE     10 10-May-84   275    512  Codefile
SHOWDEMO.CODE        6 10-May-84   285    512  Codefile
SCRIPT.TEXT         42 10-May-84   291    512  Textfile
```

```
DEMO.TEXT            8 10-May-84    333    512  Textfile
DEMO.CODE            2 10-May-84    341    512  Codefile
SYSTEM.COMPILER    107 29-Mar-84    343    512  Codefile
SYSTEM.SYNTAX       14  4-May-83    450    512  Codefile
SYSTEM.LIBRARY      41  9-Apr-84    464    512  Copefile
SYSTEM.STARTUP      12 10-May-84    505    512  Codefile
SYSTEM.WRK.TEXT      4  2-Sep-86    517    512  Textfile
SYSTEM.WRK.CODE      2  2-Sep-86    521    512  Codefile
< UNUSED >         197              523
```

10. Press the **Spacebar** twice to return to the Filer command line.

NOTE

From now on, you will not be given the step-by-step instructions to display the diskette directory on the screen. You should know that this procedure involves typing **E** from the Filer and typing either the volume number (#4:) or the volume name (usually STUDENT:).

Change a Filename. The name of a file on a disk is not always the name we want it to have. Filenames should provide a clue to the contents of the file. Sometimes our first choice for a filename is not the best and we want to change it. The Filer provides a command for just this purpose. Assume that ACCOUNTS87.TEXT would be a better name for the file you just created. To change the filename,

1. Type **C**.

The system responds:

```
Change what file ?
```

asking you which filename you wish to change.

2. Type **BUDGET87.TEXT**

The system then confirms your selection and asks what new name you would like.

```
Change what file ? BUDGET87.TEXT
Change to what ?
```

3. Type **ACCOUNTS87.TEXT** and press **Enter**.

The computer confirms the filename change.

```
Filer: G(et, S(ave, W(hat, N(ew, L(dir, R(em, C(hng, T(rans, D(ate,? [ED 1R0.0]
Change to what ? ACCOUNTS87.TEXT
STUDENT:BUDGET87.TEXT       --> ACCOUNTS87.TEXT
```

As in the M(ake command, the system refuses to accept a filename that doesn't follow the rules.

4. Verify the file change by displaying the directory again.

If you are working with the Filer and type **C** by mistake, you can press **Enter** in response to the "Change what file" question, and the system returns you to the Filer command line without changing anything.

Copy a File on the Screen Sometimes you want to print information in a file on your screen. One way to do this is to T(ransfer the file to the display screen. As an illustration, you can transfer the contents of SYSTEM.WRK.TEXT to the screen.

Review the volumes attached to your system.

1. Type **V**.

The computer displays the volumes:

```
Filer: G(et, S(ave, W(hat, N(ew, L(dir, R(em, C(hng, T(rans, D(ate,? [ED 1R0.0]
Vols on-line:
  1   CONSOLE:
  2   SYSTERM:
  4 # STUDENT: [  720]
  6   PRINTER:
  7   REMIN:
  8   REMOUT:
Root vol is - STUDENT:
Prefis is - STUDENT:
```

In the same way that files can be thought of as file folders, volumes are file cabinets. The transfer operation places a copy of the information in one file in another file. At the end of the operation, there are two copies of the information. The transfer operation does not destroy or erase the original file.

The file SYSTEM.WRK.TEXT is in volume STUDENT:. We want to display it on the screen, which has the volume name CONSOLE:. The operation, therefore, is the transfer of the file STUDENT:SYSTEM.WRK.TEXT to the volume CONSOLE:.

2. Type **T**.

The computer asks for the name of the file to transfer.

```
Transfer what file ? _
```

3. Type **SYSTEM.WRK.TEXT** and press **Enter**.

```
Transfer what file ? SYSTEM.WRK.TEXT
 To where ?
```

The computer confirms your choice and now needs to know the destination.

4. Type **CONSOLE:** and press **Enter**.

The computer now responds in two ways. The first display is the contents of SYSTEM.WRK.TEXT, which is produced by the transfer operation.

```
Filer: G(et, S(ave, W(hat, N(ew, L(dir, R(em, C(hng, T(rans, D(ate,? [ED 1R0.0]
PROGRAM FIRST;
BEGIN
    WRITE('I can do it!');
END.




STUDENT:SYSTEM.WRK.TEXT    --> CONSOLE:
```

The last line of the display is a confirmation that the transfer was completed.

Copy a File on the Disk One situation you encounter many times is having a completed project in the file SYSTEM.WRK.TEXT, and wanting to begin a new project with this file. You do, however, want to save the information stored in SYSTEM.WRK.TEXT. Therefore, before erasing SYSTEM.WRK.TEXT and beginning a new project, you can use the T(ransfer command to make a copy of your information in another disk file.

As an example, transfer the program you wrote in Module 3 to a file called CANDO.TEXT. Since the function of the program is to print "I can do it!" on the screen, CANDO.TEXT is a meaningful filename for this program.

1. Type **T** for T(ransfer.

The computer responds with

```
Transfer what file ?
```

and asks which file to transfer.

2. Type **SYSTEM.WRK.TEXT** and press **Enter**.

The computer displays

```
Transfer what file ? SYSTEM.WRK.TEXT
To where ?
```

and now needs the name of the destination file.

3. Type **CANDO.TEXT** and press **Enter.**

The disk drive will spin while the transfer takes place, and the computer will confirm the transfer by displaying:

```
Filer: G(et, S(ave, W(hat, N(ew, L(dir, R(em, C(hng, T(rans, D(ate,? [ED 1R0.0]
To where ? CANDO.TEXT
STUDENT:SYSTEM.WRK.TEXT    --> STUDENT:CANDO.TEXT
```

4. Verify that this transfer occurred by displaying the second screen of the directory on the screen and looking for your new file.

```
Filer: G(et, S(ave, W(hat, N(ew, L(dir, R(em, C(hng, T(rans, D(ate,? [ED 1R0.0]
STUDENT:
CANDO.TEXT          4  2-Sep-86   533   512  Textfile
< UNUSED >        183             537
24/24 files<listed/in-dir>, 537 blocks used, 183 unused, 183 in largest
```

F(lip Swap/Lock The Filer is contained in several segments, not all of which must be in the memory at one time. This allows the Filer to have more memory to work with and permits some operations to be performed more rapidly. However, when working with a single disk drive system (as you are, whether or not you have more than one physical disk drive) it is advisable to "lock" all of the Filer segments into memory before beginning an activity where you need to swap diskettes.

1. Type **F**.

```
Filer: G(et, S(ave, W(hat, N(ew, L(dir, R(em, C(hng, T(rans, D(ate,? [ED 1.R0.0]
Filer segments memlocked. [22275 words]
```

This display indicates the entire Filer is locked in memory. The number of available words of main memory is displayed. This number may be different for your computer.

2. Type **F**.

```
Filer: G(et, S(ave, W(hat, N(ew, L(dir, R(em, C(hng, T(rans, D(ate,? [ED 1.R0.0]
Filer segments swappable. [22275 words]
```

The same action used to lock the Filer also unlocks it so it can be swapped in and out of memory as needed. The next operations in this module involve operations requiring multiple diskettes, therefore the Filer needs to be locked in memory.

3. Type **F** to memlock the Filer.

Copy to Another Diskette A single disk is certainly not going to hold all the programs you develop. Just as the T(ransfer command allowed you to transfer a file from volume STUDENT: to volume CONSOLE:, the Transfer command also allows the transfer of files from one disk to another.

In the full p-System, this second disk could be located in another disk drive. The PC APPRENTICE version of the p-System, however, allows the use of only a single disk drive. It is still possible to copy from one diskette to another with the Transfer command.

For this example, you need a second diskette which has been formatted for data storage with the p-System. This is the diskette you formatted in preparation for the start of this module.

1. Type **T** for Transfer.

The computer responds:

```
Transfer what file ?
```

2. Type **CANDO.TEXT** and press **Enter**.

The computer responds:

```
Transfer what file ? CANDO.TEXT
To where ? _
```

3. Type **BLANK:CANDO.TEXT** and press **Enter**.

The computer responds:

```
Put in BLANK:
 Type <space> to continue _
```

4. Remove STUDENT: from the disk drive and insert BLANK:.

NOTE

If you transfer a large file from one diskette to another you need to exchange diskettes several times. The system will instruct you to swap diskettes any time this is necessary.

5. Press **Spacebar**.

The computer performs the transfer and displays the confirmation on the screen:

```
Filer: G(et, S(ave, W(hat, N(ew, L(dir, R(em, C(hng, T(rans, D(ate,? [ED 1R0.0]
Type <space> to continue
STUDENT:CANDO.TEXT          --> BLANK:CANDO.TEXT
```

6. Verify the transfer by displaying the directory of BLANK:.

```
Filer: G(et, S(ave, W(hat, N(ew, L(dir, R(em, C(hng, T(rans, D(ate,? [ED 1R0.0]
BLANK:
CANDO.TEXT          4  4-Sep-86     6   512  Textfile
< UNUSED >        710              10
1/1 files<listed/in-dir>, 10 blocks used, 710 unused, 710 in largest
```

7. Remove BLANK: from the disk drive and insert STUDENT:.
8. Display the second screen of the directory of STUDENT:.

```
Filer: G(et, S(ave, W(hat, N(ew, L(dir, R(em, C(hng, T(rans, D(ate,? [ED 1R0.0]
STUDENT:
CANDO.TEXT          4  4-Sep-86   533   512  Textfile
< UNUSED >        183             537
24/24 files<listed/in-dir>, 537 blocks used, 183 unused, 183 in largest
```

As expected, the file CANDO.TEXT is still intact on STUDENT:. There are now three total copies of this program. Copy one is called SYSTEM.WRK.TEXT, copy two is STUDENT:CANDO.TEXT, and copy three is BLANK:CANDO.TEXT.

Copy a File to the Printer You have seen that you can transfer a file to the CONSOLE: and read it on the screen. That does not allow you to carry a copy of the text with you. The T(ransfer command can also transfer a file to a printer.

CAUTION

Do not proceed with this section unless you have a printer attached to your system. Trying to transfer a file to a nonexistant printer may lock up your system and force you to turn it off and on to restart.

1. Turn on the printer.

2. Type **T** for T(ransfer.

The computer responds:

```
Transfer what file ?
```

3. Type **CANDO.TEXT** and press **Enter**.

The computer responds:

```
Filer: G(et, S(ave, W(hat, N(ew, L(dir, R(em, C(hng, T(rans, D(ate,? [ED 1R0.0]
To where ?
```

4. Type **PRINTER:** (don't forget the colon) and press **Enter**.

The printer prints your file, and the screen displays:

```
Filer: G(et, S(ave, W(hat, N(ew, L(dir, R(em, C(hng, T(rans, D(ate,? [ED 1R0.0]
To where ? PRINTER:
STUDENT:CANDO.TEXT          --> PRINTER:
```

Delete a File You have created and copied several files in this module which are no longer necessary. To prevent the disk from becoming filled with unnecessary files, the R(emove command is used to erase unwanted files.

1. Type **R** for R(emove.

The computer responds:

```
Remove what file ?
```

2. Type **ACCOUNTS87.TEXT** and press **Enter**.

The computer responds:

```
Remove what file ? ACCOUNTS87.TEXT
 STUDENT:ACCOUNTS87.TEXT    --> removed
 Update directory ? _
```

The deletion is not actually complete until you update the diskette directory. If you type anything except **Y** at this point, the file is not deleted.

3. Answer the question by typing **Y**.

WHAT YOU HAVE LEARNED

- Create (describe) filenames
- Change filenames
- Copy files to the screen
- Copy files on diskettes
- Copy files to the printer
- Erase (remove) files from the diskette

REVIEW

1. What are the only characters that can be used in a filename?

2. What kind of files can be used by the p-System Editor?

3. What does the p-System do if you include an invalid character in a filename?

4. How long can a filename be?

5. What command will permit you to create a new file on the diskette?

6. What does the p-System do if you don't specify the length of the new file?

7. What command allows you to change a filename?

8. An office file cabinet and file folder are like what parts of the p-System?

9. What command allows you to copy a file?

10. What command allows you to erase a file?

Module 6
MANAGING DISK SPACE

KEY TOPICS

- Check diskette for damage
- Consolidate unused space on the diskette

PRACTICE SESSION

Creating and changing files are only part of the skill you need to effectively use a diskette. This module teaches you how to get the most use out of the space on your diskette.

PREPARATION Your screen should display the Filer command line.

LEARNING ACTIVITY The diskette used for storage needs help from you to keep the files on it arranged in good order.

Diskettes are not a permanent storage medium because they can be physically damaged and the information lost. You can prevent most damage by using high-quality diskettes and handling them correctly, but sometimes manufacturing defects, accidents, or wear will destroy part of a diskette surface. Not all damage results in total loss of data, or makes the diskette unusable.

The p-System provides options in the Filer to assist you in recovering from errors caused by damage to the diskette. The first step is to determine that damage actually exists on the diskette.

Check Diskette for Damage. The diskette is divided into segments called *blocks*. If you think there may be something wrong with your diskette you perform a bad-blocks scan.

1. Type **?** from the first Filer screen to show the second screen of commands.

Your display shows the second Filer screen:

```
Filer: Q(uit, B(ad-blks, E(xt-dir, K(rnch, M(ake, P(refix, V(ols, ? [ED 1R0.0]
```

The second command shown on the command line is the B(ad-blks command.

2. Type **B** for B(ad-blks.

The computer responds:

```
Bad block scan of what vol ?
```

The diskette can be referred to by either its volume number, #4, its name, STUDENT:, or * for the root volume.

3. Type **#4:** to designate the disk drive.

The computer responds:

```
Bad block scan of what vol ? #4:
Scan for 720 blocks ? (Y/N)
```

This option allows you to specify exactly which portions of the diskette should be checked for bad blocks. On systems with high capacity disk drives containing thousands of blocks, you might not want to scan the entire disk. On a floppy diskette it makes sense to scan the entire diskette as the time required is not long.

4. Type **Y** to confirm the scan of the entire diskette.

The computer responds:

```
Filer: G(et, S(ave, W(hat, N(ew, L(dir, R(em, C(hng, T(rans, D(ate,? [ED 1R0.0]
Scan for 720 blocks ? (Y/N) Y
Block 6 is bad
1 bad blocks
File(s) endangered:
SYSTEM.KEY            6     7
```

If you are working with a new, high quality diskette, the system will probably report that there is one bad block, block 6. Your PC APPRENTICE diskette has been specially prepared with this bad block. This error report lists the blocks which are "bad." If this bad block is inside a file, the system warns you of the files which may contain bad blocks. For example, block 6 is bad, which puts the file SYSTEM.KEY in danger.

There are several reasons a block could be bad. Block 6 is bad because it was intentionally written that way. Other blocks may be bad because of a speck of dust or a bad spot on the disk. The Examine command attempts to fix the bad blocks. First, it exercises the mechanics of the disk drive in an attempt to dislodge any foreign material. If it is unsuccessful in doing this, it writes a bad-block file at the location of the bad block on the diskette. This prevents any valuable files from being stored where there are bad blocks.

Now that bad blocks have been identified, you can attempt to fix them so that the system will not store files there. This is done with the Examine command.

5. Type **??** to see the third screen of Filer commands.

```
Filer: X(amine, Z(ero, O(n/off-line, F(lip-swap/lock [ED 1R).0]
```

6. Type **X** to examine the bad blocks.

```
Examine blocks on what vol ? _
```

7. Type **#4:** and press **Enter** to indicate the disk drive.

```
Examine blocks on what vol ? #4:
Block-range ? _
```

8. Type **6-6** and press **Enter.**

The screen displays:

```
File(s) endangered:
SYSTEM.KEY            6   7
Fix them ? _
```

9. Type **Y.**

```
Filer: G(et, S(ave, W(hat, N(ew, L(dir, R(em, C(hng, T(rans, D(ate,? [ED 1R0.0]
```

Because this block isn't actually bad, nothing has happened. If you do have a bad block on your diskette, the filer will create a file called BAD.00000.BAD of type "Bad file" on your diskette. This prevents any valuable information from being stored on a bad place on the diskette.

Consolidate Unused Space on the Diskette After performing a number of disk operations, editing new files, deleting files, copying files, and so forth. the UNUSED space on the disk becomes fragmented. When this happens, there may be plenty of space available for a new file you need but, because it is not all together on the disk, there is not enough room for the new file. The K(runch command moves all the files on the disk together so that the unused space all ends up at the end of the disk. The K(runch command has no effect on bad-block files which were created with the Examine command.

1. Type **K** to crunch your diskette.

The system responds:

```
Crunch what vol ? _
```

2. Type **#4:** and press **Enter**.

The system responds:

```
Crunch what vol ? #4:
From end of disk, block 720  ? (Y/N) _
```

3. Type **Y** to confirm crunching the entire diskette.

The system will keep you informed of its progress by displaying the names of the files it moves. It does not move all the files, just the ones which are separated by unused space.

```
Filer: G(et, S(ave, W(hat, N(ew, L(dir, R(em, C(hng, T(rans, D(ate,? [ED 1R0.0]
Moving forward CANDO.TEXT
STUDENT: crunched
```

4. Display the directory on the screen.

```
Type <space> to continue
STUDENT:
SYSTEM.KEY          1 27-Apr-84    6   512  Datafile
SYSTEM.PASCAL     102 26-Apr-84    7   512  Datafile
SYSTEM.IBM.86      24 14-Feb-84  109   512  Datafile
SYSTEM.CONFIG      17  2-Sep-84  133   512  Datafile
SYSTEM.MISCINFO     1  2-Apr-84  150   226  Datafile
SYSTEM.FONT         2  4-Jan-84  151   512  Datafile
SYSTEM.FILER       39 26-Mar-84  153   512  Codefile
SYSTEM.EDITOR      51 26-Mar-84  192   512  Codefile
PRINT.CODE         17 14-Dec-82  243   512  Codefile
CONFIGURE.CODE     13 10-May-84  260   512  Codefile
LOGO.FONT           2 25-Apr-84  273   512  Datafile
DISKFORMAT.CODE    10 10-May-84  275   512  Codefile
SHOWDEMO.CODE       6 10-May-84  285   512  Codefile
SCRIPT.TEXT        42 10-May-84  291   512  Textfile
DEMO.TEXT           8 10-May-84  333   512  Textfile
```

```
DEMO.CODE           2 10-May-84    341    512  Codefile
SYSTEM.COMPILER   107 29-Mar-84    343    512  Codefile
SYSTEM.SYNTAX      14  4-May-83    450    512  Codefile
SYSTEM.LIBRARY     41  9-Apr-84    464    512  Copefile
SYSTEM.STARTUP     12 10-May-84    505    512  Codefile
SYSTEM.WRK.TEXT     4  2-Sep-86    517    512  Textfile
SYSTEM.WRK.CODE     2  2-Sep-86    521    512  Codefile
BUDGET87.TEXT      10  2-Sep-86    523    512  Textfile
```

5. Press the **Spacebar** to display the second screen.

```
Filer: G(et, S(ave, W(hat, N(ew, L(dir, R(em, C(hng, T(rans, D(ate,? [ED 1R0.0]
STUDENT:
< UNUSED >          193                    527
23/23 files<listed/in-dir>, 527 blocks used, 193 unused, 193 in largest
```

All of the files have been placed together at the beginning of the diskette, and the unused space has been put at the end. The only exception is that if you have a bad-block file, it is not moved.

WHAT YOU HAVE LEARNED

- Check (scan) for damage on the diskette
- Consolidate (crunch) files on the diskette

REVIEW

1. What problems can diskettes develop?

2. What is one way to minimize problems with diskettes?

3. What is the command to check a diskette for damage?

4. When would you not want to scan an entire disk?

5. How does the p-System inform you of the existence of a bad block?

6. How does the p-System correct a bad block?

7. What is the command to consolidate the files on a diskette?

8. Why would you want to consolidate the unused space on a diskette?

PART 4
INTRODUCTION TO EDITING

WHAT YOU WILL LEARN

- Clear workfile
- Insert text
- Delete text
- Exchange text
- Move text
- Copy text
- Adjust text
- Abort changes

Module 7
CHANGING TEXT

KEY TOPICS

- Clear workfile
- Insert text
- Delete text
- Exchange text
- Move text
- Copy text
- Adjust text
- Abort changes

PRACTICE SESSION

Much of what you do on the computer will involve using text in some way. It is important that you become as proficient as possible in working with text, so you can take full advantage of the options in the p-System.

PREPARATION You should know by now that you need to have your system running and have the STUDENT: diskette in the disk drive. You will be expected to start the system without being reminded.

LEARNING ACTIVITY You should have the main command line of the p-System displayed on your computer screen.

```
Command: E(dit, R(un, F(ile, C(omp, X(ecute, U(ser restart [ED 1R0.0]
```

Clearing Workfile The p-System has a workfile already created for you to use. You learned in an earlier module that this workfile is called SYSTEM.WRK.TEXT. You access this workfile from the Editor.

1. Type **E** to start the Editor.

The computer responds:

```
>Edit: A(djust C(opy D(el F(ind I(nsert J(ump K(ol M(argin P(age ? [ED 1R0.0]
PROGRAM FIRST;
BEGIN
    WRITE('I can do it!');
END.
```

The computer has read your old program from the diskette and placed it in the Editor's workspace. In the last module, you copied this material from SYSTEM.WRK.TEXT to CANDO.TEXT and you no further need to keep this text in SYSTEM.WRK.TEXT. The first step, therefore, in beginning a new project is to get rid of the old project. To do this you will have to leave the Editor for a moment and use the Filer.

2. Type **Q** to quit the Editor.

The computer responds with four exit options:

```
>Quit:
     U(pdate the workfile and leave
     E(xit without updating
     R(eturn to the editor without updating
     W(rite to a file name and return
```

There is no reason to update a file you are about to erase, so exit without updating.

3. Type **E** to E(xit without updating.

This places you back at the command line:

```
Command: E(dit, R(un, F(ile, C(omp, X(ecute, U(ser restart [ED 1R0.0]
```

4. Type **F** to enter the Filer.

```
Filer: G(et, S(ave, W(hat, N(ew, L(dir, R(em, C(hng, T(rans, D(ate,? [ED 1.r0.0]
```

The fourth command on the Filer command line is "N(ew." This command is used to clear SYSTEM.WRK.TEXT so you can begin a new project.

5. Type **N** for N(ew.

```
Throw away current workfile ? _
```

6. Type **Y** to confirm this selection.

```
Filer: G(et, S(ave, W(hat, N(ew, L(dir, R(em, C(hng, T(rans, D(ate,? [ED 1.r0.0]
Workfile cleared
```

The computer confirms that it has cleared the workfile (SYSTEM.WRK.TEXT) and is ready to begin a new project.

7. Type **Q** to quit the Filer.

The computer returns you to the main command line.

```
Command: E(dit, R(un, F(ile, C(omp, X(ecute, U(ser restart [ED 1R0.0]
```

Inserting Text The workfile is cleared and the system is ready to begin a new project. Start your new project by entering the Editor.

1. Type **E** for the Editor.

```
>Edit:
No workfile is present. File? ( <ret> for no file ) _
```

The computer confirms that no workfile is present. It is possible to edit a file other than SYSTEM.WRK.TEXT by typing its name at this point. However, do not do so at this time.

2. Press **Enter** to use SYSTEM.WRK.TEXT as the Editor workfile.

```
>Edit: A(djust C(opy D(el F(ind I(nsert J(ump K(ol M(argin P(age ? [ED 1R0.0]
```

The Editor is not particular about what type of material you place in your textfile. In this module, you practice editing with the following short poem:

Twinkle, twinkle, little star.
How I wonder what you are.
Up above the world so high
Like a diamond in the sky.
Twinkle, twinkle, little star.
How I wonder what you are.

3. Type **I** to enter the insert mode.

```
>Insert: Text {<bs> a char, <del> a line} [<etx> accepts, <esc> escapes]
```

The Insert command line contains some shorthand notes to remind you of the functions available in Insert mode. The first function is the entry of text. Pressing any alphabetic, numeric, or special symbol on the keyboard will insert that character into the text where the cursor is positioned.

If you make a mistake in the Insert mode a mistake is made, you can correct the error without leaving Insert. The reminder "{<bs> a char" means that pressing **Backspace** once deletes a single character.

Your first impression might be "<del> a line" means pressing the **Del** key located in the lower right-hand corner of your keyboard deletes a line. The **Ins** and **Del** keys are not used in the Insert mode. The "<del>" function is activated by pressing **Ctrl- Backspace**. As a result, all deletions in the Insert mode are done with the **Backspace** or **Ctrl-Backspace** combination.

The text you type in the Insert mode is temporarily placed in the workspace. You can either keep the insertion or throw it away. These two options are shown in shorthand as "{<etx> accepts, <esc> escapes}."

The escape option returns the workspace to the condition it was in before you pressed **I** for insert. This option is activated by pressing the **Esc** key on the keyboard.

CAUTION

If you accidentally press **Esc** while in Insert you will lose everything you typed since entering the Insert mode. It is a good idea to press **Ctrl-C** frequently and re-enter Insert to prevent this sort of accident.

A careful examination of your keyboard will not reveal a key marked **Etx**. There is no **Etx** key. This function is activated by pressing **Ctrl-C**.

4. Type the first two lines of the poem; press **Enter** after each line:

```
>Insert: Text {<bs> a char, <del> a line} [<etx> accepts, <esc> escapes]
 Twinkle, twinkle, little star.
 How I wonder what you are.

 _
```

5. Use the **Backspace** key to correct any errors you have made.

6. When your text matches the sample above, press **Ctrl-C** to accept the insertion.

```
>Edit: A(djust C(opy D(el F(ind I(nsert J(ump K(ol M(argin P(age ? [ED 1R0.0]
Twinkle, twinkle, little star.
How I wonder what you are.

_
```

The first two lines of the poem have now been accepted from temporary insertion into the Editor's workspace.

Delete Text Sometimes you will change your mind about text after accepting the insertion. It is always possible to change what is in the Editor's workspace. Nothing is permanent.

1. Press **I** to enter I(nsert.

```
>Insert: Text {<bs> a char, <del> a line} [<etx> accepts, <esc> escapes]
 Twinkle, twinkle, little star.
 How I wonder what you are.
```

2. Type the next two lines of the poem **exactly** as written below, including the errors.

   Down below the ocean low.
   Like a codfish in the atmosphere.

```
>Insert: Text {<bs> a char, <del> a line} [<etx> accepts, <esc> escapes]
Twinkle, twinkle, little star.
How I wonder what you are.
Down below the ocean low.
Like a codfish in the atmosphere.
```

3. Press **Ctrl-C** to accept your insertion.

The original version of the poem is certainly more inspiring than the version on the screen. To change the wording to conform to the standard version you need to delete some text.

The cursor marks the place in the text where deletions will occur. Use the **Up Arrow**, **Down Arrow**, **Left Arrow**, and **Right Arrow** keys on the **8**, **2**, **4**, and **6** keys on the numeric keypad to move the cursor up, down, left, and right.

NOTE

If the "arrow" keys do not appear to work, you may have accidentally pressed the **Num Lock** key. Press **Num Lock** to restore the movement function of these keys.

4. Move the cursor until it is under the "D" in "Down" in the third line of the poem.

```
>Edit: A(djust C(opy D(el F(ind I(nsert J(ump K(ol M(argin P(age ? [ED 1R0.0]
Twinkle, twinkle, little star.
How I wonder what you are.
Down below the ocean low.
Like a codfish in the atmosphere.
```

5. Type **D** for D(elete.

```
>Delete: < > <moving commands> {<etx> to delete, <esc> to abort}
Twinkle, twinkle, little star.
How I wonder what you are.
Down below the ocean low.
Like a codfish in the atmosphere.
```

Any movement of the cursor will delete the text the cursor passes. An entire line of text can be deleted by pressing **Enter**.

6. Press **Enter** twice.

```
>Delete: < > <moving commands> {<etx> to delete, <esc> to abort}
Twinkle, twinkle, little star.
How I wonder what you are.
```

You have deleted more of the poem than necessary. As in the insert mode, you now have the option of accepting or rejecting your deletion. Because more text than necessary was deleted, reject the deletion.

7. Press **Esc** to reject the deletion.

```
>Edit: A(djust C(opy D(el F(ind I(nsert J(ump K(ol M(argin P(age ? [ED 1R0.0]
Twinkle, twinkle, little star.
How I wonder what you are.
Down below the ocean low.
Like a codfish in the atmosphere.
```

The workspace is returned to exactly the same condition it was before you typed **D**, including the position of the cursor under the "D." Just delete one line this time.

8. Type **D** for D(elete.

```
>Delete: < > <moving commands> {<etx> to delete, <esc> to abort}
Twinkle, twinkle, little star.
How I wonder what you are.
Down below the ocean low.
Like a codfish in the atmosphere.
```

9. Press **Enter** once.

```
>Delete: < > <moving commands> {<etx> to delete, <esc> to abort}
Twinkle, twinkle, little star.
How I wonder what you are.

Like a codfish in the atmosphere.
```

The third line of text has disappeared.

10. Press **Ctrl-C** to accept the deletion.

```
>Edit: A(djust C(opy D(el F(ind I(nsert J(ump K(ol M(argin P(age ? [ED 1R0.0]
Twinkle, twinkle, little star.
How I wonder what you are.
Like a codfish in the atmosphere.
```

The text has been reformatted on the screen to fill in the space left by your deletion.

You can also delete by the character instead of by the line.

11. Use the cursor control keys to place the cursor under the "a" in "atmosphere."

```
>Edit: A(djust C(opy D(el F(ind I(nsert J(ump K(ol M(argin P(age ? [ED 1R0.0]
Twinkle, twinkle, little star.
How I wonder what you are.
Like a codfish in the atmosphere.
```

12. Type **D** for Delete.

```
>Delete: < > <moving commands> {<etx> to delete, <esc> to abort}
Twinkle, twinkle, little star.
How I wonder what you are.
Like a codfish in the atmosphere.
```

Any cursor movement away from the cursor's present location deletes text.

13. Press the **Backspace** key twice.

```
>Delete: < > <moving commands> {<etx> to delete, <esc> to abort}
Twinkle, twinkle, little star.
How I wonder what you are.
Like a codfish in th_ atmosphere.
```

You have deleted part of the word "the." You can recover from inadvertent deletions by moving the cursor in the other direction.

14. Press the **Spacebar** twice to restore the previous display.

```
>Delete: < > <moving commands> {<etx> to delete, <esc> to abort}
Twinkle, twinkle, little star.
How I wonder what you are.
Like a codfish in the atmosphere.
```

Your incorrect deletion has been restored. Now delete the word "atmosphere."

15. Press the **spacebar** five times to delete the "atmos" in "atmosphere."

```
>Delete: < > <moving commands> {<etx> to delete, <esc> to abort}
Twinkle, twinkle, little star.
How I wonder what you are.
Like a codfish in the      phere.
```

16. Press the **Right Arrow** five times to delete the "phere" in "atmosphere."

```
>Delete: < > <moving commands> {<etx> to delete, <esc> to abort}
Twinkle, twinkle, little star.
How I wonder what you are.
Like a codfish in the           .
```

Both the **Spacebar** and the **Right Arrow** perform the forward character delete function in the Delete mode. You can use the one you prefer.

17. Press **Ctrl-C** to accept the deletion.

```
>Edit: A(djust C(opy D(el F(ind I(nsert J(ump K(ol M(argin P(age ? [ED 1R0.0]
Twinkle, twinkle, little star.
How I wonder what you are.
Like a codfish in the .
```

More Insertions Most of the incorrect text is gone from the poem. Before correcting "codfish," use the insertion procedure to insert the word "sky" at the end of the last line.

1. Type **I** for insert.

2. Type **sky**.

3. Press **Ctrl-C**.

```
>Edit: A(djust C(opy D(el F(ind I(nsert J(ump K(ol M(argin P(age ? [ED 1R0.0]
Twinkle, twinkle, little star.
How I wonder what you are.
Like a codfish in the sky._
```

4. Press **Up Arrow** and **Right Arrow** one time to place the cursor at the end of the second line.

5. Type **I** for Insert.

6. Press **Enter**.

```
>Insert: Text {<bs> a char, <del> a line} [<etx> accepts, <esc> escapes]
Twinkle, twinkle, little star.
How I wonder what you are.
```

The last line of the poem has disappeared! Don't worry, though; it will be restored shortly. It has simply been moved to make room for your insertion.

7. Type **Up above the world so high** and press **Ctrl-C**.

```
>Edit: A(djust C(opy D(el F(ind I(nsert J(ump K(ol M(argin P(age ? [ED 1R0.0]
Twinkle, twinkly, little star.
How I wonder what you are.
Up above the world so high_
Like a codfish in the sky.
```

The insertion is accepted, and the last line of the poem has been restored in its proper position.

Exchange Text Deleting incorrect text, accepting the deletion, inserting correct text, and accepting the insertion is not the only way to correct errors. It is possible to perform both functions at once with the exchange command.

1. Use the cursor control keys to place the cursor under the "c" in "codfish."

2. Type **?** to view the second screen of Editor commands.

```
>Edit: Q(uit R(plc S(et V(erify X(ch Z(ap [ED 1R0.0]
 Twinkle, twinkle, little star.
 How I wonder what you are.
 Up above the world so high
 Like a codfish in the sky.
```

You do not have to be able to view the command to use it, but the reminder is reassuring.

3. Type **X** for exchange.

```
>eXchange: Text <vector keys> {<etx>,<esc> CURRENT line}
Twinkle, twinkle, little star.
How I wonder what you are.
Up above the world so high
Like a codfish in the sky.
```

In the Exchange mode, anything you type will replace what is already on the screen.

4. Type **diamond.**

5. Press **Ctrl-C** to accept the exchange.

```
>Edit: A(djust C(opy D(el F(ind I(nsert J(ump K(ol M(argin P(age ? [ED 1R0.0]
Twinkle, twinkle, little star.
How I wonder what you are.
Up above the world so high
Like a diamond_in the sky.
```

This was a simple operation because "codfish" and "diamond" have the same number of letters. If the number of letters is different, you need to use Exchange in combination with the **Ins** and **Del** keys. As you gain experience with the Editor, you will discover the combination of commands that works best for you in each situation.

Move Text The first two lines of the poem are the same as the last two lines. Instead of typing these lines again, you can move them as a block. Moving text relies on the fact that the Editor remembers your last deletion or insertion when you delete or insert text. All text which is deleted is stored temporarily in a copy buffer. This is what allows you to change your mind about deletions. It also makes moves possible.

1. Place the cursor at the end of the poem, just past the word "sky."
2. Type **I** for insert.
3. Press **Enter**.
4. Press **Ctrl-C**.

You have inserted a blank line at the end of your workspace.

5. Place the cursor under the "T" in the first "Twinkle" on the first line of the poem.
6. Type **D** for delete.
7. Press **Enter** twice.
8. Press **Ctrl-C** to accept your deletion.

```
>Edit: A(djust C(opy D(el F(ind I(nsert J(ump K(ol M(argin P(age ? [ED 1R0.0]
Up above the world so high
Like a diamond in the sky.
```

The first two lines of the poem are gone but not forgotten.

9. Move the cursor to the end of the poem, on the blank line, directly below the "L" in "Like."

```
>Edit: A(djust C(opy D(el F(ind I(nsert J(ump K(ol M(argin P(age ? [ED 1R0.0]
 Up above the world so high.
 Like a diamond in the sky.

 _
```

10. Type **C** for Copy.

11. Type **B** for Buffer.

```
>Edit: A(djust C(opy D(el F(ind I(nsert J(ump K(ol M(argin P(age ? [ED 1R0.0]
Up above the world so high
Like a diamond in the sky.
Twinkle, twinkle, little star.
How I wonder what you are.
```

Copy Text The move operation was successful in moving the text from the top of the poem to the bottom, but the poem calls for it to appear in both places. The operation needed is a copy which will leave the original intact.

1. Place the cursor under the "T" in the first "Twinkle."

2. Type **D** for Delete.

3. Press **Enter** twice.

4. Press **Esc** to cancel the deletion.

This time you have not actually deleted anything, but you have loaded the last two lines of the poem into the buffer.

5. Move the cursor under the "U" in "Up."

6. Type **C** for Copy.

7. Type **B** for Buffer.

```
>Edit: A(djust C(opy D(el F(ind I(nsert J(ump K(ol M(argin P(age ? [ED 1R0.0]
 Twinkle, twinkle, little star.
 How I wonder what you are.
 Up above the world so high
 Like a diamond in the sky.
 Twinkle, twinkle, little star.
 How I wonder what you are.
```

Adjust Text Now that the poem is complete, you could dress up its appearance on the screen with some creative indenting.

1. Place the cursor under the "H" in "How."

2. Type **A** for Adjust.

```
>Adjust: L(just R(just C(enter <arrow keys> {<etx> to leave}
 Twinkle, twinkle, little star.
 How I wonder what you are.
 Up above the world so high
 Like a diamond in the sky.
 Twinkle, twinkle, little star.
 How I wonder what you are.
```

3. Press the **Right Arrow** twice.

4. Press the **Down Arrow** once to place the cursor on the next line.

5. Press the **Right Arrow** twice to move the third line over.

```
>Adjust: L(just R(just C(enter <arrow keys> {<etx> to leave}
 Twinkle, twinkle, little star.
   How I wonder what you are.
     Up above the world so high
 Like a diamond in the sky.
 Twinkle, twinkle, little star.
 How I wonder what you are.
```

6. Press the **Down Arrow**.

7. Press the **Right Arrow** twice.

8. Press the **Down Arrow**.

9. Press the **Right Arrow** twice.

```
>Adjust: L(just R(just C(enter <arrow keys> {<etx> to leave}
 Twinkle, twinkle, little star.
   How I wonder what you are.
      Up above the world so high
         Like a diamond in the sky.
            Twinkle, twinkle, little star.
 How I wonder what you are.
```

10. Press the **Down Arrow** key.

11. Press the **Right Arrow** twice.

12. Press **Ctrl-C** to accept the adjustments.

```
>Edit: A(djust C(opy D(el F(ind I(nsert J(ump K(ol M(argin P(age ?  [ED 1R0.0]
Twinkle, twinkle, little star.
   How I wonder what you are.
      Up above the world so high
         Like a diamond in the sky.
            Twinkle, twinkle, little star.
               How I wonder what you are.
```

Another possibility for attractive formatting of the poem would be to center each line on the screen.

13. Type **A** for Adjust.

14. Type **C** for Center.

15. Press the **Up Arrow** five times.

16. Press **Ctrl-C** to accept your adjustment.

```
>Edit: A(djust C(opy D(el F(ind I(nsert J(ump K(ol M(argin P(age ? [ED 1R0.0]
                        Twinkle, twinkle, little star.
                          How I wonder what you are.
                          Up above the world so high
                          Like a diamond in the sky.
                        Twinkle, twinkle, little star.
                          How I wonder what you are.
```

Save Your Work. Before going on, save your work to protect yourself against power failures and other hazards.

1. Type **Q** for Quit.

```
>Quit:
     U(pdate the workfile and leave
     E(xit without updating
     R(eturn to the editor without updating
     W(rite to a file name and return
```

2. Type **U** to update the workfile and return to the command line.

```
Command: E(dit, R(un, F(ile, C(omp, X(ecute, U(ser restart [ED 1R0.0]
```

WHAT YOU HAVE LEARNED

- Clear workfile
- Insert text
- Delete text
- Exchange text
- Move text
- Copy text
- Adjust text
- Abort changes

REVIEW

1. Which Filer command will clear SYSTEM.WRK.TEXT?

2. Which command line would you use to insert text?

3. How can you delete a character while in Insert?

4. How do you delete a line while in Insert?

5. What key combination activates the Accept Insertion command?

6. Which key will start the Delete mode?

7. How should you move the cursor to recover from an accidental deletion?

8. Which keys are normally used to move the cursor?

9. Which command allows you to exchange text?

10. Where is the text you delete stored?

11. What command allows you to duplicate text in another location?

12. What command allows you to adjust text?

PART 5
MORE EDITING

WHAT YOU WILL LEARN

- Change Editor direction indicator
- Move by page
- Cursor movement
- Find
- Replace

Module 8
MOVING THROUGH THE WORKSPACE

KEY TOPICS

- Change Editor direction indicator
- Move by Page
- Cursor movement
- Find
- Replace

PRACTICE SESSION

In this module you are going to learn additional ways to move through text. When you have large amounts of text to change or edit these procedures will be very helpful.

PREPARATION From the main p-System command line type **E** to enter the Editor. Your display should look like this:

```
>Edit: A(djust C(opy D(el F(ind I(nsert J(ump K(ol M(argin P(age ? [ED 1R0.0]
                    Twinkle, twinkle, little star.
                      How I wonder what you are.
                      Up above the world so high
                      Like a diamond in the sky.
                    Twinkle, twinkle, little star.
                      How I wonder what you are.
```

To illustrate some of the methods available for you to move through the workspace, you need to have some additional practice text. Instead of typing text, you can create a large amount of practice text quickly using the Copy command.

1. Type **D** for Delete.

2. Press **Enter** six times.

3. Press **CTRL-C**.

4. Press key sequence **CB** five times for copy from buffer.

Your screen now displays:

```
>Edit: A(djust C(opy D(el F(ind I(nsert J(ump K(ol M(argin P(age ? [ED 1R0.0]
                              Twinkle, twinkle, little star.
                                How I wonder what you are.
                                Up above the world so high
                                Like a diamond in the sky.
                              Twinkle, twinkle, little star.
                                How I wonder what you are.
                              Twinkle, twinkle, little star.
                                How I wonder what you are.
                                Up above the world so high
                                Like a diamond in the sky.
                              Twinkle, twinkle, little star.
                                How I wonder what you are.
```

5. Type **I** for Insert.

6. Type **This is the last line in the workspace.**

7. Press **Ctrl-C** to accept your insertion.

You have created five copies of the poem. Only the last two copies appear on the screen. The first three copies are hidden off the top of the screen.

LEARNING ACTIVITY The Editor has several commands that allow you to move the cursor through the workspace without affecting the text.

Jump Your cursor is presently at the bottom of the workspace.

1. Press and hold the **Up Arrow** until the cursor moves to the top of the workspace.

Moving through five copies didn't take long, but if there were 50 copies it would be a time-consuming task. The Editor provides a command to jump to the beginning or end of the file immediately.

2. Type **J** for jump.

```
>JUMP: B)eginning E)nd M)arker <esc>_
                              Twinkle, twinkle, little star.
                                How I wonder what you are.
                                Up above the world so high
                                Like a diamond in the sky.
                              Twinkle, twinkle, little star.
                                How I wonder what you are.
                              Twinkle, twinkle, little star.
                                How I wonder what you are.
                                Up above the world so high
                                Like a diamond in the sky.
                              Twinkle, twinkle, little star.
                                How I wonder what you are.
                              Twinkle, twinkle, little star.
                                How I wonder what you are.
                                Up above the world so high
                                Like a diamond in the sky.
                              Twinkle, twinkle, little star.
                                How I wonder what you are.
                              Twinkle, twinkle, little star.
                                How I wonder what you are.
                                Up above the world so high
                                Like a diamond in the sky.
                              Twinkle, twinkle, little star.
                                How I wonder what you are.
```

3. Type **E** for End-of-workspace.

```
>Edit: A(djust C(opy D(el F(ind I(nsert J(ump K(ol M(argin P(age ? [ED 1R0.0]
                                Up above the world so high
                                Like a diamond in the sky.
                              Twinkle, twinkle, little star.
                                How I wonder what you are.
                              Twinkle, twinkle, little star.
                                How I wonder what you are.
                                Up above the world so high
                                Like a diamond in the sky.
                              Twinkle, twinkle, little star.
                                How I wonder what you are.
                              Twinkle, twinkle, little star.
```

```
          How I wonder what you are.
          Up above the world so high
          Like a diamond in the sky.
        Twinkle, twinkle, little star.
          How I wonder what you are.
        Twinkle, twinkle, little star.
          How I wonder what you are.
          Up above the world so high
          Like a diamond in the sky.
        Twinkle, twinkle, little star.
          How I wonder what you are.
This is the last line of the workspace._
```

With two keystrokes, you have placed the cursor at the end of the workspace.

4. Type **J** for Jump.

5. Type **B** for Beginning.

```
>Edit: A(djust C(opy D(el F(ind I(nsert J(ump K(ol M(argin P(age ? [ED 1R0.0]
                     Twinkle, twinkle, little star.
                       How I wonder what you are.
                       Up above the world so high
                       Like a diamond in the sky.
                     Twinkle, twinkle, little star.
                       How I wonder what you are.
                     Twinkle, twinkle, little star.
                       How I wonder what you are.
                       Up above the world so high
                       Like a diamond in the sky.
                     Twinkle, twinkle, little star.
                       How I wonder what you are.
                     Twinkle, twinkle, little star.
                       How I wonder what you are.
                       Up above the world so high
                       Like a diamond in the sky.
                     Twinkle, twinkle, little star.
                       How I wonder what you are.
                     Twinkle, twinkle, little star.
                       How I wonder what you are.
                       Up above the world so high
                       Like a diamond in the sky.
                     Twinkle, twinkle, little star.
                       How I wonder what you are.
```

The cursor is now located at the beginning of the workspace.

Direction Indicator Look at the upper left corner of the Editor screen. There is a ">" immediately before the word "Edit." This symbol is the Editor direction indicator. When you start the Editor, the direction indicator is pointing forward (>) toward the end of the workspace.

1. Press **Enter** ten times.

The cursor travels down ten lines of text.

2. Type **<**, located on the same key as the comma.

```
<Edit: A(djust C(opy D(el F(ind I(nsert J(ump K(ol M(argin P(age ? [ED 1R0.0]
                        Twinkle, twinkle, little star.
                          How I wonder what you are.
                          Up above the world so high
                          Like a diamond in the sky.
                        Twinkle, twinkle, little star.
                          How I wonder what you are.
                        Twinkle, twinkle, little star.
                          How I wonder what you are.
                          Up above the world so high
                          Like a diamond in the sky.
                        Twinkle, Twinkle little star.
                          How I wonder what you are.
                        Twinkle, twinkle, little star.
                          How I wonder what you are.
                          Up above the world so high
                          Like a diamond in the sky.
                        Twinkle, twinkle, little star.
                          How I wonder what you are.
                        Twinkle, twinkle, little star.
                          How I wonder what you are.
                          Up above the world so high
                          Like a diamond in the sky.
                        Twinkle, twinkle, little star.
                          How I wonder what you are.
```

3. Press **Enter**.

Notice that this time the cursor moved *up* a line.

4. Press **Enter** five times.

The cursor continues to move up.

5. Type **>**.

The direction indicator in the upper left corner of the screen changes direction again.

```
>Edit: A(djust C(opy D(el F(ind I(nsert J(ump K(ol M(argin P(age ? [ED 1R0.0]
                          Twinkle, twinkle, little star.
                            How I wonder what you are.
                            Up above the world so high
                            Like a diamond in the sky.
                          Twinkle, Twinkle little star.
                            How I wonder what you are.
                          Twinkle, twinkle, little star.
                            How I wonder what you are.
                            Up above the world so high
                            Like a diamond in the sky.
                          Twinkle, twinkle, little star.
                            How I wonder what you are.
                          Twinkle, twinkle, little star.
                            How I wonder what you are.
                            Up above the world so high
                            Like a diamond in the sky.
                          Twinkle, twinkle, little star.
                            How I wonder what you are.
                          Twinkle, twinkle, little star.
                            How I wonder what you are.
                            Up above the world so high
                            Like a diamond in the sky.
                          Twinkle, twinkle, little star.
                            How I wonder what you are.
```

You can use the < and > keys at any time in the Editor to change the Editor direction indicator.

NOTE

It is not necessary to press the **Shift** key when typing < or > to change the direction indicator. The comma and period keys have the same effect.

Page Movement It is possible to move through the workspace a screenful of lines at a time using the Page command.

1. Type **P**.

```
>Edit: A(djust C(opy D(el F(ind I(nsert J(ump K(ol M(argin P(age ? [ED 1R0.0]
                          Twinkle, twinkle, little star.
                            How I wonder what you are.
                            Up above the world so high
                            Like a diamond in the sky.
                          Twinkle, Twinkle little star.
                            How I wonder what you are.
This is the last line of the workspace.
```

You have advanced to the next page of text.

2. Type **P** again.

The screen display is the same, except that the cursor is now at the end of the workspace. You cannot page beyond the end of the workspace.

3. Type < to change the direction indicator.

4. Type **P** twice to move the cursor to the beginning of the workspace.

```
>Edit: A(djust C(opy D(el F(ind I(nsert J(ump K(ol M(argin P(age ? [ED 1R0.0]
                          Twinkle, twinkle, little star.
                            How I wonder what you are.
                            Up above the world so high
                            Like a diamond in the sky.
                          Twinkle, twinkle, little star.
                            How I wonder what you are.
                          Twinkle, twinkle, little star.
                            How I wonder what you are.
                            Up above the world so high
                            Like a diamond in the sky.
                          Twinkle, twinkle, little star.
                            How I wonder what you are.
                          Twinkle, twinkle, little star.
                            How I wonder what you are.
```

```
Up above the world so high
Like a diamond in the sky.
Twinkle, twinkle, little star.
How I wonder what you are.
Twinkle, twinkle, little star.
How I wonder what you are.
Up above the world so high
Like a diamond in the sky.
Twinkle, twinkle, little star.
How I wonder what you are.
```

The direction indicator determines in which direction to page with the page command. You can page both forward and backward through the workspace.

Find Text The purpose of the F(ind command is to locate a specific word or phrase of text. As an example, find the word "sky" in your text.

1. Type **F** for Find.

```
<Find[1]: L(it <target> =>_
Twinkle, twinkle, little star.
How I wonder what you are.
Up above the world so high
Like a diamond in the sky.
Twinkle, twinkle, little star.
How I wonder what you are.
Twinkle, twinkle, little star.
How I wonder what you are.
Up above the world so high
Like a diamond in the sky.
Twinkle, twinkle, little star.
How I wonder what you are.
Twinkle, twinkle, little star.
How I wonder what you are.
Up above the world so high
Like a diamond in the sky.
Twinkle, twinkle, little star.
How I wonder what you are.
Twinkle, twinkle, little star.
How I wonder what you are.
Up above the world so high
Like a diamond in the sky.
Twinkle, twinkle, little star.
How I wonder what you are.
```

The Editor requires a "target" to find. This target must begin and end with a delimiter, a special character used to enclose the target word. The delimiter can be any special character not used in the text, such as /, **@**, or **&**.

2. Type **/sky/** since our target word is "sky."

```
ERROR: Pattern not in the file  Please press <spacebar> to continue.
                        Twinkle, twinkle, little star.
                          How I wonder what you are.
                          Up above the world so high
                          Like a diamond in the sky.
                        Twinkle, twinkle, little star.
                          How I wonder what you are.
                        Twinkle, twinkle, little star.
                          How I wonder what you are.
                          Up above the world so high
                          Like a diamond in the sky.
                        Twinkle, twinkle, little star.
                          How I wonder what you are.
                        Twinkle, twinkle, little star.
                          How I wonder what you are.
                          Up above the world so high
                          Like a diamond in the sky.
                        Twinkle, twinkle, little star.
                          How I wonder what you are.
                        Twinkle, twinkle, little star.
                          How I wonder what you are.
                          Up above the world so high
                          Like a diamond in the sky.
                        Twinkle, twinkle, little star.
                          How I wonder what you are.
```

Why did this happen? You can see the word "sky" on the screen in four locations. Did the Editor make a mistake? Not likely.

3. Press the **spacebar**.

```
<Edit: A(djust C(opy D(el F(ind I(nsert J(ump K(ol M(argin P(age ? [ED 1R0.0]
                    Twinkle, twinkle, little star.
                      How I wonder what you are.
                      Up above the world so high
                      Like a diamond in the sky.
                    Twinkle, twinkle, little star.
                      How I wonder what you are.
                    Twinkle, twinkle, little star.
                      How I wonder what you are.
                      Up above the world so high
                      Like a diamond in the sky.
                    Twinkle, twinkle, little star.
                      How I wonder what you are.
                    Twinkle, twinkle, little star.
                      How I wonder what you are.
                      Up above the world so high
                      Like a diamond in the sky.
                    Twinkle, twinkle, little star.
                      How I wonder what you are.
                    Twinkle, twinkle, little star.
                      How I wonder what you are.
                      Up above the world so high
                      Like a diamond in the sky.
                    Twinkle, twinkle, little star.
                      How I wonder what you are.
```

Look at the Editor direction indicator. The command you gave the Editor was "Start looking for 'sky' between where the cursor is located and the beginning of the file." Since the cursor was already at the beginning, there was no place to look. If the cursor had been at the end of the workspace, this command would have located the last occurrence of "sky" in the workspace.

4. Type **>** to point the direction indicator forward.

5. Type **F** for Find.

6. Type /**sky**/.

```
>Edit: A(djust C(opy D(el F(ind I(nsert J(ump K(ol M(argin P(age ? [ED 1R0.0]
                    Twinkle, twinkle, little star.
                      How I wonder what you are.
                      Up above the world so high
                      Like a diamond in the sky.
                    Twinkle, twinkle, little star.
                      How I wonder what you are.
                    Twinkle, twinkle, little star.
                      How I wonder what you are.
                      Up above the world so high
                      Like a diamond in the sky.
                    Twinkle, twinkle, little star.
                      How I wonder what you are.
                    Twinkle, twinkle, little star.
                      How I wonder what you are.
                      Up above the world so high
                      Like a diamond in the sky.
                    Twinkle, twinkle, little star.
                      How I wonder what you are.
                    Twinkle, twinkle, little star.
                      How I wonder what you are.
                      Up above the world so high
                      Like a diamond in the sky.
                    Twinkle, twinkle, little star.
                      How I wonder what you are.
```

The command really does work. It found the first occurrence of "sky" in the text. Now find the next one.

7. Type **F** for Find.

The Editor remembers that the last thing you looked for was "/sky/." It is not necessary to retype this literal string.

8. Type **S** for Same.

```
>Edit: A(djust C(opy D(el F(ind I(nsert J(ump K(ol M(argin P(age ? [ED 1R0.0]
                    Twinkle, twinkle, little star.
                      How I wonder what you are.
                      Up above the world so high
                      Like a diamond in the sky.
                    Twinkle, twinkle, little star.
                      How I wonder what you are.
                    Twinkle, twinkle, little star.
                      How I wonder what you are.
                      Up above the world so high
                      Like a diamond in the sky.
                    Twinkle, twinkle, little star.
                      How I wonder what you are.
                    Twinkle, twinkle, little star.
                      How I wonder what you are.
                      Up above the world so high
                      Like a diamond in the sky.
                    Twinkle, twinkle, little star.
                      How I wonder what you are.
                    Twinkle, twinkle, little star.
                      How I wonder what you are.
                      Up above the world so high
                      Like a diamond in the sky.
                    Twinkle, twinkle, little star.
                      How I wonder what you are.
```

Replace Finding a pattern of text is useful, but it would be more useful if we could change the text as well. This is done much like finding a pattern of text.

1. Type **JB** to jump to the beginning of the text.

This will allow you to find and replace through the entire workspace.

Let's find the word "Twinkle" and replace it with "Gargle."

2. Type **R** for Replace.

```
>Replace[1]: L(it V(fy <targ> <sub>  =>_
                         Twinkle, twinkle, little star.
                           How I wonder what you are.
                           Up above the world so high
                           Like a diamond in the sky.
                         Twinkle, twinkle, little star.
                           How I wonder what you are.
                         Twinkle, twinkle, little star.
                           How I wonder what you are.
                           Up above the world so high
                           Like a diamond in the sky.
                         Twinkle, twinkle, little star.
                           How I wonder what you are.
                         Twinkle, twinkle, little star.
                           How I wonder what you are.
                           Up above the world so high
                           Like a diamond in the sky.
                         Twinkle, twinkle, little star.
                           How I wonder what you are.
                         Twinkle, twinkle, little star.
                           How I wonder what you are.
                           Up above the world so high
                           Like a diamond in the sky.
                         Twinkle, twinkle, little star.
                           How I wonder what you are.
```

3. Type **/Twinkle/ / Gargle/**.

"Twinkle" and "twinkle" are two separate target patterns. Use a capital "T."

```
>Edit: A(djust C(opy D(el F(ind I(nsert J(ump K(ol M(argin P(age ? [ED 1R0.0]
                         Gargle, twinkle, little star.
                           How I wonder what you are.
                           Up above the world so high
                           Like a diamond in the sky.
                         Twinkle, twinkle, little star.
                           How I wonder what you are.
                         Twinkle, twinkle, little star.
                           How I wonder what you are.
```

```
Up above the world so high
Like a diamond in the sky.
Twinkle, twinkle, little star.
How I wonder what you are.
Twinkle, twinkle, little star.
How I wonder what you are.
Up above the world so high
Like a diamond in the sky.
Twinkle, twinkle, little star.
How I wonder what you are.
Twinkle, twinkle, little star.
How I wonder what you are.
Up above the world so high
Like a diamond in the sky.
Twinkle, twinkle, little star.
How I wonder what you are.
```

4. Type **5R** for Replace five times.

```
>Replace[5]: L(it V(fy <targ> <sub>  =>_
                        Gargle, twinkle, little star.
                          How I wonder what you are.
                          Up above the world so high
                          Like a diamond in the sky.
                        Twinkle, twinkle, little star.
                          How I wonder what you are.
                        Twinkle, twinkle, little star.
                          How I wonder what you are.
                          Up above the world so high
                          Like a diamond in the sky.
                        Twinkle, twinkle, little star.
                          How I wonder what you are.
                        Twinkle, twinkle, little star.
                          How I wonder what you are.
                          Up above the world so high
                          Like a diamond in the sky.
                        Twinkle, twinkle, little star.
                          How I wonder what you are.
                        Twinkle, twinkle, little star.
                          How I wonder what you are.
                          Up above the world so high
                          Like a diamond in the sky.
                        Twinkle, twinkle, little star.
                          How I wonder what you are.
```

5. Type **/Twinkle/ / Gargle/** to do the same replacement five more times.

```
>Edit: A(djust C(opy D(el F(ind I(nsert J(ump K(ol M(argin P(age ? [ED 1R0.0]
                    Gargle, twinkle, little star.
                      How I wonder what you are.
                    Gargle, twinkle, little star.
                      How I wonder what you are.
                      Up above the world so high
                      Like a diamond in the sky.
                    Gargle, twinkle, little star.
                      How I wonder what you are.
                    Gargle, twinkle, little star.
                      How I wonder what you are.
                      Up above the world so high
                      Like a diamond in the sky.
                    Gargle, twinkle, little star.
                      How I wonder what you are.
                    Twinkle, twinkle, little star.
                      How I wonder what you are.
                      Up above the world so high
                      Like a diamond in the sky.
                    Twinkle, twinkle, little star.
                      How I wonder what you are.
                    Twinkle, twinkle, little star.
                      How I wonder what you are.
                      Up above the world so high
                      Like a diamond in the sky.
```

It appears that the replacement was only performed four times. There are only five "Gargles" on the screen. What has actually happened is that the top of the workspace is off the screen.

6. Type **JB** to jump to the beginning of the workspace and count the "Gargles" again.

7. Type **/R** for "Replace as many times as possible."

8. Type **/Twinkle/ / Gargle/** to specify the replacement.

```
>Edit: A(djust C(opy D(el F(ind I(nsert J(ump K(ol M(argin P(age ? [ED 1R0.0]
                         Gargle, twinkle, little star.
                           How I wonder what you are.
                         Gargle, twinkle, little star.
                           How I wonder what you are.
                           Up above the world so high
                           Like a diamond in the sky.
                         Gargle, twinkle, little star.
                           How I wonder what you are.
                         Gargle, twinkle, little star.
                           How I wonder what you are.
                           Up above the world so high
                           Like a diamond in the sky.
                         Gargle, twinkle, little star.
                           How I wonder what you are.
This is the last line in the workspace.
```

All the "Twinkles" are replaced by "Gargles."

9. Quit the Editor, Exit without updating, and return to the command line.

WHAT YOU HAVE LEARNED

- Change Editor direction indicator
- Move by page
- Cursor movement
- Find
- Replace

REVIEW

1. What does the J(ump command permit you to do with your text?

2. Where is the direction indicator located?

3. How do you change the direction indicator?

4. What does changing the direction indicator allow you to do in the text?

5. What command allows you to move through the text by pages?

6. What command sets you up to locate a specific part of the text?

7. What is a delimiter and what is its purpose?

8. What command allows you to replace text after finding it?

9. How do you specify a specific number of times for a replacement?

10. How do you specify replacement everywhere in the workspace?

PART 6
BEGINNING PROGRAMMING

WHAT YOU WILL LEARN

- Create a program
- Correct Compiler errors
- Create literal output
- Position literal output

Module 9
PROGRAM SHELL

KEY TOPICS

- Create a program
- Correct Compiler errors

PRACTICE SESSION

Now you are ready to begin learning how to create useful Pascal programs. Creating a simple yet practical program requires that you follow the programming syntax rules.

PREPARATION Enter the Filer from the main command line. Select the **N** option to clear the workfile, and respond to the verification message with a **Y**. Use the **D** option to reset the system date. **K**(runch your diskette. **Q**(uit the Filer, returning to the main command line.

LEARNING ACTIVITY A computer program is a set of statements which the computer can follow to carry out a task. You have already used several programs in this course. The p-System is a computer program to allow the computer to communicate with the disk drive, keyboard, monitor, and printer. The Editor is a program to create and change text and store it on the disk. The Filer is a program to manage disk files. The Compiler is a program to translate Pascal programs into p-Code which the computer can understand. In Modules 3 and 4 you created a Pascal program and ran it. With the exception of complexity, there is little difference between this program and the Editor, Filer, and Compiler. All are sets of instructions for the computer to follow. In fact, all of the major components of the p-System are written in the Pascal programming language.

The language we speak, English, is too complex and unclear in meaning to be understood by a computer program. The binary language of zeros and ones of the machine's natural language is not easily understood by humans. Computer programming languages, such as Pascal, have been developed to bridge this gap between a natural language for man and a natural language for machine. A computer language contains Englishlike words and mathematical symbols familiar to humans, but the words and symbols are arranged according to rigid rules of structure and syntax to make their meaning understandable to machines.

1. Type **F** to enter the Filer.

```
Filer:  G(et, S(ave, W(hat, N(ew, L(dir, R(em, C(hng, T(rans, D(ate,? [ED 1.R0.0]
```

The fourth command on the Filer command line is "N(ew." This command is used to clear SYSTEM.WRK.TEXT so you can begin a new project.

2. Type **N** for N(ew.

```
Throw away current workfile ? _
```

3. Type **Y** to confirm this selection.

```
Filer: G(et, S(ave, W(hat, N(ew, L(dir, R(em, C(hng, T(rans, D(ate,? [ED 1.r0.0]
Workfile cleared
```

The computer confirms that it has cleared the workfile (SYSTEM.WRK.TEXT) and is ready to begin a new project.

4. Type **Q** to quit the Filer.

```
Command: E(dit, R(un, F(ile, C(omp, X(ecute, U(ser restart [ED 1R0.0]
```

5. Type **E** to enter the Editor.

6. Type **I** for insert.

```
>Edit: A(djust C(opy D(el F(ind I(nsert J(ump K(ol M(argin P(age ? [ED 1R0.0]
PROGRAM SHELL;
BEGIN
END.
```

7. Type the following program:

   PROGRAM SHELL;
   BEGIN
   END.

8. Press **Ctrl-C** to accept the insertion.

```
>Edit: A(djust C(opy D(el F(ind I(nsert J(ump K(ol M(argin P(age ? [ED 1R0.0]
PROGRAM SHELL;
BEGIN
END.
```

The PROGRAM statement identifies this text as a program and gives the program a name. The computer will not accept a program that doesn't have a name. This program is named SHELL. It could have been named "GERFUNK," but SHELL is more meaningful. The second statement, BEGIN, marks the beginning of the statements the computer will follow. The END statement marks the end of the program. Notice that the END statement is followed by a period.

The computer is strict in its enforcement of the rules of syntax. An error as small as forgetting the period at the end of the program will prevent the computer from understanding your program.

Recovering from Typing Errors It is inevitable that eventually you will make an error in typing a program. To illustrate the procedure for correcting an error, make the following error in your program.

1. Use the cursor control keys to place the cursor under the "G" in the word "BEGIN."

2. Type **X** for exchange.

3. Type **K** to form the word BEKIN.

4. Press **Ctrl-C** to accept the exchange.

5. Type **QU** to quit the Editor and Update the workfile.

6. Type **R** to run the program.

```
Compiling...
Output file for compiled listing? (<cr> for none)
```

7. Press **Enter**.

```
Compiling...
Output file for compiled listing? (<cr> for none)

Pascal compiler - release level [ED 1R0.0-2]
<     0>...
PROGRAM SHELL;
BEKIN <---
Error in declaration part
Line 2
Type <sp> to continue, <esc> to terminate, or 'e' to edit
```

The last line of this display gives you three options.

a. The message "type <sp> to continue" means that you can press the **Spacebar** to have the Compiler continue to look for errors in the rest of the program.

b. The message "<esc> to terminate" means that you can stop compiling the program and return to the command line.

c. The message "'e' for edit" means that you can go immediately to the Editor.

8. Type **E** to return to the Editor.

The computer places the cursor at the end of the word BEKIN because that was the point at which it discovered the error. Taking the "e" option from the Compiler error screen is useful in pointing out the location of errors.

9. Press the **Spacebar** to Enter the edit mode.

```
>Edit: A(djust C(opy D(el F(ind I(nsert J(ump K(ol M(argin P(age ? [ED 1R0.0]
PROGRAM SHELL;
BEKIN
END.
```

The Edit command line reappears, and you are in the Editor.

10. Use the Editor to change the “K” back to a “G.”

11. Quit the Editor, Update the workfile, and Run the program.

```
Command: E(dit, R(un, F(ile, C(omp, X(ecute, U(ser restart [ED 1R0.0]
Running...
```

The computer returns to the command line. Your correction is successful.

WHAT YOU HAVE LEARNED

- Create a program
- Correct Compiler errors

REVIEW

1. All text entry in the Editor must be done in what mode?

2. Every Pascal program must have at least what three statememts?

3. Which command tells the computer to compile and execute program statements?

4. What mode must you work from to correct typing errors by typing over the incorrect text?

Module 10
OUTPUT STATEMENTS

KEY TOPICS

- Create literal output
- Position literal output

PRACTICE SESSION

The most basic statement available is the output statement. Without output, computer programs are useless.

PREPARATION The computer should display the main command line of the p-System.

LEARNING ACTIVITY For a program to be useful, it must perform a function. One of the most basic functions is the production of text on the screen. The Pascal statements WRITE and WRITELN are used to produce output on the screen.

Recall your program from the previous module.

1. Type **E** for Edit.

```
>Edit: A(djust C(opy D(el F(ind I(nsert J(ump K(ol M(argin P(age ? [ED 1R0.0]
PROGRAM SHELL;
BEGIN
END.
```

The name "SHELL" is not appropriate for a meaningful program. In this module, you will again work with the poem "Twinkle, Twinkle, Little Star." The program name "TWINKLE" is a better name for the program.

2. Use the Editor commands to change the name of the program from "SHELL" to "TWINKLE."

```
>Edit: A(djust C(opy D(el F(ind I(nsert J(ump K(ol M(argin P(age ? [ED 1R0.0]  \
PROGRAM TWINKLE;
BEGIN
END.
```

Create Literal Output In the first modules, you used the WRITE statement to place the words "I can do it!" on the screen. Now, use the WRITE statement to place the first two lines of the poem on the screen.

1. Use the cursor control keys to place the cursor after the "N" in "BEGIN."

2. Press **I** for Insert.

3. Press **Enter** to begin a new line of text.

```
>Insert: Text {<bs> a char, <del> a line} [<ext> accepts, <esc> escapes]
PROGRAM TWINKLE;
BEGIN
```

Don't worry that the last line of the program has disappeared. It will be restored when you have completed the insertion.

The cursor is positioned immediately under the "B" in "BEGIN." When you press **Enter**, the Editor assumes you wish to begin the next line in the same column as the previous one. Indentations in the program text make the program more readable.

4. Press the **Spacebar** four times to indent the next line of text four spaces.

5. Type **WRITE ('Twinkle, twinkle, little star.');** and press **Enter**.

```
>Insert: Text {<bs> a char, <del> a line} [<ext> accepts, <esc> escapes]
PROGRAM TWINKLE
BEGIN
    WRITE ('Twinkle, twinkle, little star.');
    _
```

The cursor returns to the position immediately below the "W."

6. Type **WRITE ('How I wonder what you are.');**.
7. Press **Ctrl-C** to accept the insertion.

```
>Edit: A(djust C(opy D(el F(ind I(nsert J(ump K(ol M(argin P(age ? [ED 1R0.0]
PROGRAM TWINKLE
BEGIN
    WRITE ('Twinkle, twinkle, little star.');
    WRITE ('How I wonder what you are.');
END.
```

The "END." has returned to the last line of your program. Check your text carefully against the screen display above. Have you forgotten a semicolon? If so, use the Editor commands to correct your error now, before you save and compile.

8. Quit the Editor, Update the workfile, and Run the program.

```
Command: E(dit, R(un, F(ile, C(omp, X(ecute, U(ser restart [ED 1R0.0]
Running...
Twinkle, Twinkle Little Star.How I wonder what you are.
```

The output is all there, but it is not arranged the way poems are written. The second WRITE statement places the second line of the poem immediately following the first line; it didn't even leave a space.

Position Literal Output You need to give the computer a different command to force it to begin a new line after printing. The WRITELN statement performs this function. It is identical to the WRITE statement, except that it ends the current line and directs the computer to place any additional output on the next line.

1. Type **E** to enter the Editor.

2. Place the cursor on the space immediately following the first "WRITE."

```
>Insert: Text {<bs> a char, <del> a line} [<ext> accepts, <esc> escapes]
PROGRAM TWINKLE;
BEGIN
    WRITE_                                              ('Twinkle, twinkle, little star.');
    WRITE ('How I wonder what you are.');
END.
```

The rest of the line is moved to the right to make room for your insertion.

4. Type **LN** and press **Ctrl-C** to accept the insertion.

```
>Edit: A(djust C(opy D(el F(ind I(nsert J(ump K(ol M(argin P(age ? [ED 1R0.0]
PROGRAM TWINKLE;
BEGIN
    WRITELN_('Twinkle, twinkle, little star.');
    WRITE ('How I wonder what you are.');
END.
```

The remainder of the line takes its place where it belongs.

5. Repeat the insertion procedure for the second WRITE statement.

```
>Edit: A(djust C(opy D(el F(ind I(nsert J(ump K(ol M(argin P(age ? [ED 1R0.0]
PROGRAM TWINKLE;
BEGIN
    WRITELN ('Twinkle, twinkle, little star.');
    WRITELN_('How I wonder what you are.');
END.
```

NOTE

You need to perform the operations of **Q**(uit the Editor, **U**(pdate the workfile, **R**(un the program, and press **Enter**, frequently to run your programs. You are now familiar with these operations so that future instructions will simply instruct you to run the program. It is assumed that you will follow the process of quitting the Editor and updating the workfile.

6. Run the program.

```
Command: E(dit, R(un, F(ile, C(omp, X(ecute, U(ser restart [ED 1R0.0]
Running...
Twinkle, twinkle, little star.
How I wonder what you are.
```

The WRITELN statement places the second line of the poem directly under the first, where it belongs!

7. Enter the Editor, recalling your program to the screen.

```
>Edit: A(djust C(opy D(el F(ind I(nsert J(ump K(ol M(argin P(age ? [ED 1R0.0]
PROGRAM TWINKLE;
BEGIN
    WRITELN ('Twinkle, twinkle, little star.');
    WRITELN ('How I wonder what you are.');
END.
```

Put the third line of the poem on the screen the hard way, then take the easy route for the fourth line.

8. Insert the statements in your program as shown. Spaces are important inside the quotations! Be careful to get the spaces exactly as printed.

WRITE ('Up ');
WRITE ('above ');
WRITE ('the');
WRITE (' world ');
WRITELN ('so high');
WRITELN ('Like a diamond in the sky.');

```
>Edit: A(djust C(opy D(el F(ind I(nsert J(ump K(ol M(argin P(age ? [ED 1R0.0]
PROGRAM TWINKLE;
BEGIN
    WRITELN ('Twinkle, twinkle, little star.');
    WRITELN ('How I wonder what you are.');
    WRITE ('Up ');
    WRITE ('above ');
    WRITE ('the');
    WRITE (' world ');
    WRITELN ('so high');
    WRITELN ('Like a diamond in the sky.');
END.
```

9. Run the program.

```
Command: E(dit, R(un, F(ile, C(omp, X(ecute, U(ser restart [ED 1R0.0]
Running...
Twinkle, twinkle, little star.
How I wonder what you are.
Up above the world so high
Like a diamond in the sky.
```

The poem appears on the screen on four lines, as it should. The WRITELN statements begin a new line where needed. If your screen is different, use the Editor to double check the spacing in the WRITE statements, then run the program again.

WHAT YOU HAVE LEARNED

- Create literal output
- Position literal output

REVIEW

1. What two Pascal statements produce output on the monitor?

2. If you press **Enter** after typing a program line, where will the cursor move?

3. What symbol is used to separate Pascal statements?

4. How is the WRITELN statement different from the WRITE statement?

5. What happens to the output when spaces are included between quotation marks as in the output list?

PART 7
COMPILE AND EXECUTE

WHAT YOU WILL LEARN

- Comments and Compiler directives
- Create Compiler listing
- Quiet compile option
- Compile-time errors
- Executing programs

Module 11
THE COMPILER

KEY TOPICS

- Comments and Compiler directives
- Create Compiler listing
- Quiet Compile option
- Compile-time errors

PRACTICE SESSION

Understanding the Compiler and how it functions makes you a more effective programmer and makes it easier to correct some of the problems you may encounter.

PREPARATION Set the date; crunch the diskette and return to the main command line of the p-System.

LEARNING ACTIVITY The Pascal Compiler is a computer program that translates your Pascal textfile into the p-code the computer can understand.

The Compiler has several options to make your program development faster and simpler. Placing these options in the program text instructs the Compiler to behave differently.

Comments and Compiler Directives As the programs you write become more and more complicated, you need to add explanations in English to explain the meaning of your program text. This is done by enclosing your comments in a matched set of brackets: {This is a comment.}. With one exception, the Compiler ignores anything enclosed between brackets. The text enclosed in brackets is included any time you list your program, but the Compiler does not attempt to translate it into p-code.

The exception to the rule that anything in brackets is ignored is when the first character following the opening bracket, {, is a dollar sign, $. In this case, the Compiler interprets this as a Compiler directive, which is an instruction to the Compiler on how to compile the program. Several of these Compiler directives are explained in the next section.

Create Compiler Listing with L+ There are several ways to look at your program text. You have learned how to T(ransfer the file SYSTEM.WRK.TEXT to the CONSOLE: or to the PRINTER:. The Compiler is capable of providing you with another type of listing. It contains all the information in SYSTEM.WRK.TEXT, plus additional information which will be useful to you in correcting errors. The listing is placed in a file called SYSTEM.LST.TEXT on your diskette. The Compiler does not create this file without your instructions. Follow the procedure below to produce a listing file called SYSTEM.LST.TEXT.

1. Type **E** to start the Editor.

Your program appears on the screen:

```
>Edit: A(djust C(opy D(el F(ind I(nsert J(ump K(ol M(argin P(age ? [ED 1R0.0]
PROGRAM TWINKLE;
BEGIN
   WRITELN ('Twinkle, twinkle, little star.');
   WRITELN ('How I wonder what you are.');
   WRITE ('Up ');
   WRITE ('above ');
   WRITE ('the');
   WRITE (' world ');
   WRITELN ('so high');
   WRITELN ('Like a diamond in the sky.');
END.
```

Use the Editor to add the line {$L+} as the first line in your file.

2. Place the cursor under the "P" in "PROGRAM," then type **I** for Insert.

```
>Insert: Text {<bs> a char, <del> a line} [<ext> accepts, <esc> escapes]
                                                        PROGRAM TWINKLE;
BEGIN
   WRITELN ('Twinkle, twinkle, little star.');
   WRITELN ('How I wonder what you are.');
   WRITE ('Up ');
   WRITE ('above ');
   WRITE ('the');
   WRITE ('world ');
   WRITELN ('so high');
   WRITELN ('Like a diamond in the sky.');
END.
```

3. Type {**$L+**} and press **Enter** to move "PROGRAM" to the next line.

4. Press **Ctrl-C** to accept your insertion.

```
>Edit: A(djust C(opy D(el F(ind I(nsert J(ump K(ol M(argin P(age ? [ED 1R0.0]
{$L+}
PROGRAM TWINKLE
BEGIN
    WRITELN ('Twinkle, twinkle, little star.');
    WRITELN ('How I wonder what you are.');
    WRITE ('Up ');
    WRITE ('above ');
    WRITE ('the');
    WRITE ('world ');
    WRITELN ('so high');
    WRITELN ('Like a diamond in the sky.');
END.
```

5. Run the program.

6. Press **Enter** in response to the "Output file for Compiler listing" question.

```
Command: E(dit, R(un, F(ile, C(omp, X(ecute, U(ser restart [ED 1R0.0]
Running...
Twinkle, twinkle, little star.
How I wonder what you are.
Up above the world so high
Like a diamond in the sky.
```

The program compiles and runs as it did before. The instructions you added have no effect on the program's output. There is a difference, however.

7. Use the the Filer to display the files on the diskette.

```
Filer: G(et, S(ave, W(hat, N(ew, L(dir, R(em, C(hng, T(rans, D(ate,? [ED 1.r0.0]
STUDENT:
SYSTEM.WRK.CODE    2  7-Sep-86   531   512  Codefile
< UNUSED >       140             533
SYSTEM.LST.TEXT    4  7-Sep-86   673   512  Textfile
< UNUSED >        43             677
24/24 files<listed/in-dir>, 531 blocks used, 189 unused, 140 in largest
```

There is a new file on your diskette called SYSTEM.LST.TEXT. There are four ways to look at its contents:

a. Transfer SYSTEM.LST.TEXT to CONSOLE:.
b. Transfer SYSTEM.LST.TEXT to PRINTER:.
c. Use the Editor to edit SYSTEM.LST.TEXT.
d. Print it with the PRINT utility program.

8. Use the T(ransfer command to transfer SYSTEM.LST.TEXT to CONSOLE:.

```
Filer: G(et, S(ave, W(hat, N(ew, L(dir, R(em, C(hng, T(rans, D(ate,? [ED 1.r0.0]
Pascal Compiler [ED 1R0.0]-2     9/07/86
      Page   1


    1   0    0:d    1  {$L+}
    2   2    1:d    1  PROGRAM TWINKLE;
    3   2    1:0    0  BEGIN
    4   2    1:0    0      WRITELN ('Twinkle, twinkle, little star.');
    5   2    1:1   20      WRITELN ('How I wonder what you are.');
    6   2    1:1   40      WRITE ('Up ');
    7   2    1:1   53      WRITE ('above ');
    8   2    1:1   66      WRITE ('the');
    9   2    1:1   79      WRITE (' world ');
   10   2    1:1   92      WRITELN ('so high.');
   11   2    1:1  112      WRITELN ('Like a diamond in the sky.');
   12   2     :0    0  END.

End of Compilation.


 STUDENT:SYSTEM.LST.TEXT  --> CONSOLE:
```

The first column of numbers is the line number. The second column of numbers is the segment number. The third column of numbers is the routine number followed by the "lex level." The fourth column of numbers is the amount of data or code storage the routine requires at that point.

It is not important that you understand the meaning of these numbers now, or even later. However, if you make certain kinds of mistakes in your programs, the error message will refer to these numbers in identifying the location of the error. If you get an error message that refers to these numbers, simply match up the numbers in the error message with the numbers in the listing to find the location of your error.

9. If you have a printer, use the T(ransfer command to transfer SYSTEM.LST.TEXT to PRINTER:.

Turn the Listing Off As you develop longer programs, the listing will not fit on a single screen. The Compiler must also perform extra work to create the listing, which takes more time to complete the compilation. If you only need a Compiler listing of part of your program, the listing switch "{$L" can be used to turn the listing on and off: If you use both the L+ and Q+ options at the same time, Compiler errors are not printed on the screen. They only appear in the Compiler listing file.

- {$L+} turns the listing option On.
- {$L–} turns the listing option Off.

You can use these two commands as many times as you like in your program to turn the listing on and off.

1. Use the Editor to modify your program as shown:

```
>Edit: A(djust C(opy D(el F(ind I(nsert J(ump K(ol M(argin P(age ? [ED 1R0.0]
{$L+}
PROGRAM TWINKLE;
BEGIN
    WRITELN ('Twinkle, twinkle, little star.');
    {$L-}
    WRITELN (How I wonder what you are.');
    WRITE ('Up ');
    WRITE ('above ');
    WRITE ('the');
    {$L+}
    WRITE (' world ');
    WRITELN ('so high,');
    WRITELN ('Like a diamond in the sky.');
END.
```

You already know how the program looks when it runs; all you are interested in is the Compiler listing. Therefore, instead of typing **R** for Run from the command line, type **C** for C(ompile.

2. Compile the program.

3. Transfer SYSTEM.LST.TEXT to the CONSOLE:.

```
Filer: G(et, S(ave, W(hat, N(ew, L(dir, R(em, C(hng, T(rans, D(ate,? [ED 1.r0.0]
Pascal Compiler [ED 1R0.0]-2      3/22/84
      Page   1


    1   0    0:d     1  {$L+}
    2   2    1:d     1  PROGRAM TWINKLE;
    3   2    1:0     0  BEGIN
    4   2    1:1     0      WRITELN ('Twinkle, twinkle, little star.');
   10   2    1:1    20      {$L+}
   11   2    1:1    79      WRITE (' world ');
   12   2    1:1    92      WRITELN ('so high.');
   13   2    1:1   112      WRITELN ('Like a diamond in the sky');
   14   2     :0     0  END.

End of Compilation


STUDENT:SYSTEM.LST.TEXT  --> CONSOLE:
```

Compare this listing with the previous one. Notice that the lines between "{$L–}" and "{$L+}" are not in the listing.

The Listing Question Every time you compile, the Compiler asks, "Output file for compiled listing? (<cr> for none)." You have responded to this question by pressing **Enter**. If you want your Compiler listing to be placed in a file other than SYSTEM.LST.TEXT, you can specify the file name in response to this question.

1. Type **C** for Compile.

2. Type **MYLISTING.TEXT** as the name of the output file and press **Enter**.

3. Use the Filer to transfer MYLISTING.TEXT to the CONSOLE:.

```
Filer: G(et, S(ave, W(hat, N(ew, L(dir, R(em, C(hng, T(rans, D(ate,? [ED 1.r0.0]
Pascal Compiler [ED 1R0.0]-2      3/22/84
      Page   1


    1   0    0:d    1  {$L+}
    2   2    1:d    1  PROGRAM TWINKLE;
    3   2    1:0    0  BEGIN
    4   2    1:1    0      WRITELN ('Twinkle, twinkle, little star.');
   10   2    1:1   20      {$L+}
   11   2    1:1   79      WRITE (' world ');
   12   2    1:1   92      WRITELN ('so high.');
   13   2    1:1  112      WRITELN ('Like a diamond in the sky');
   14   2     :0    0  END.

End of Compilation


STUDENT:MYLISTING.TEXT  --> CONSOLE:
```

Notice that this is the same listing as you got before from SYSTEM.LST.TEXT.

One of the useful applications of this procedure is a shortcut to producing a printed listing if you have the luxury of compiling your program on a computer connected to a printer. In response to the question "Output file for Compiler listing" you can type PRINTER: to send the Compiler listing directly to the printer without placing it in a disk file first.

Title Compiler Output On one-page listings, the name of the program can be seen at the top of the page. On long programs, it is sometimes useful to have the name of the program, or the programmer, on every page of the listing. Another Compiler "switch" provides this feature. Placing "{$T My Program Title}" in your Pascal program directs the Compiler to print "My Program Title" at the top of each page, starting with the second page. You can have more than one "{$T }" statement in your program if you want different parts to have different titles.

Quiet Compile Option While the Compiler is working, it sends status messages to the CONSOLE:. If you don't want to look at these messages, or want part or all of your program to compile slightly faster, you can use the Quiet Compile option. A {$Q+} tells the Compiler to stop sending status messages to the CONSOLE:. A {$Q–} starts sending the messages. The Compiler automatically begins in the {Q–} mode. The Compiler can be told to stop sending status messages with the {Q+} switch and to start sending messages again with {$Q–}.

1. Enter the Editor.

2. Remove the {$L+} and {$L–} options from the text.

3. Turn on the quiet compile option as shown.

```
>Edit: A(djust C(opy D(el F(ind I(nsert J(ump K(ol M(argin P(age ? [ED 1R0.0]
{$Q+}
PROGRAM TWINKLE
BEGIN
    WRITELN ('Twinkle, twinkle, little star.');
    WRITELN ('How I wonder what you are.');
    WRITE ('Up ');
    WRITE ('above ');
    WRITE ('the');
    WRITE ('world ');
    WRITELN ('so high');
    WRITELN ('Like a diamond in the sky.');
END.
```

4. Compile the program

```
Compiling
Output file for compiled listing? (<cr> for none)

Pascal Compiler - release level [ED 1R0.0-2]
<    0>
```

The Compiler does not place the status messages on the screen. If there was an error, the Compiler would print the error message.

If you use both the L+ and Q+ options at the same time, Compiler errors are not printed on the screen. They only appear in the Compiler listing file.

General Compile Until this point, you have always worked with the file SYSTEM.WRK.TEXT as your text file. It is possible to work with files other than SYSTEM.WRK.TEXT.

1. Enter the Filer.

2. C(hange the name of SYSTEM.WRK.TEXT to TWINKLE.TEXT.

```
Filer: G(et, S(ave, W(hat, N(ew, L(dir, R(em, C(hng, T(rans, D(ate,? [ED 1.r0.0]
Change to what ? TWINKLE.TEXT
Remove old STUDENT:TWINKLE.TEXT ? Y
STUDENT:SYSTEM.WRK.TEXT    --> TWINKLE.TEXT
```

3. R(emove SYSTEM.WRK.CODE and update the directory.

4. Type **G** for G(et.

```
Throw away current workfile ?
```

5. Type **Y** to confirm.

```
Throw away current workfile ? Y
Get what file ?
```

6. Type **TWINKLE** and press **Enter**.

```
Filer: G(et, S(ave, W(hat, N(ew, L(dir, R(em, C(hng, T(rans, D(ate,? [ED 1.r0.0]
Get what file ? TWINKLE
Text and code file loaded
```

7. Type **Q** to quit the filer.

8. Type **C** for compile and press **Enter**.

The Compiler is now compiling the file TWINKLE.TEXT. Let's see what it has done!

9. Display the diskette directory on the screen.

```
Type <space> to continue
STUDENT:
SYSTEM.KEY          1 27-Apr-84    6   512   Datafile
SYSTEM.PASCAL     102 26-Apr-84    7   512   Datafile
SYSTEM.IBM.86      24 14-Feb-84  109   512   Datafile
SYSTEM.CONFIG      17  2-Sep-84  133   512   Datafile
SYSTEM.MISCINFO     1  2-Apr-84  150   226   Datafile
SYSTEM.FONT         2  4-Jan-84  151   512   Datafile
SYSTEM.FILER       39 26-Mar-84  153   512   Codefile
SYSTEM.EDITOR      51 26-Mar-84  192   512   Codefile
PRINT.CODE         17 14-Dec-82  243   512   Codefile
CONFIGURE.CODE     13 10-May-84  260   512   Codefile
LOGO.FONT           2 25-Apr-84  273   512   Datafile
DISKFORMAT.CODE    10 10-May-84  275   512   Codefile
SHOWDEMO.CODE       6 10-May-84  285   512   Codefile
SCRIPT.TEXT        42 10-May-84  291   512   Textfile
DEMO.CODE           2 10-May-84  333   512   Textfile
SYSTEM.COMPILER   107 29-Mar-84  341   512   Codefile
SYSTEM.SYNTAX      14  4-May-83  343   512   Codefile
SYSTEM.LIBRARY     41  9-Apr-84  450   512   Textfile
SYSTEM.STARTUP     12 10-May-84  464   512   Codefile
CANDO.TEXT          4  2-Sep-86  517   512   Codefile
TWINKLE.TEXT        4  7-Sep-86  521   512   Codefile
SYSTEM.WRK.CODE     2  7-Sep-86  525   512   Codefile
20/20 files<listed/in-dir>, 517 blocks used, 203 unused, 203 in largest
```

10. Press the **Spacebar**.

```
Filer: G(et, S(ave, W(hat, N(ew, L(dir, R(em, C(han, T(rans, D(ate,? [ED 1.r0.0]
STUDENT:
< UNUSED >        145              527
SYSTEM.LST.TEST     4  7-Sep-86    672   512   Textfile
< UNUSED >         44              676
24/24 files<listed/in-dir>, 531 blocks used, 189 unused, 145 in largest
```

The file SYSTEM.WRK.CODE is back on the diskette. The Compiler has compiled the file TWINKLE.TEXT and placed the p-code in the file SYSTEM.WRK.CODE.

11. C(hange SYSTEM.WRK.CODE to TWINKLE.CODE.

WHAT YOU HAVE LEARNED

- Comments and Compiler directives
- Create Compiler Listing
- Quiet Compile Option
- Compile-time errors

REVIEW

1. What is the value of SYSTEM.LST.TEXT?

2. What is the Compiler directive to create SYSTEM.LST.TEXT?

3. At what point can you specify that a listing be placed in a file other than SYSTEM.LST.TEXT?

4. How can your program listing be sent directly to the printer?

5. What does the {$Q+} Compiler command do?

6. What does the Compiler command {$T CHEESE INVENTORY} do?

7. How can you turn off the printing of error messages?

8. How can you add English explanations to your program?

9. Of what advantage are English explanations?

Module 12
EXECUTING PROGRAMS

KEY TOPICS

- Executing programs

PRACTICE SESSION

In your program development activities you have used the R(un command to execute the current workfile program. When the development process is complete, your program becomes ready to be used outside of the workfile environment. At this point, the program is usually Executed rather than R(un.

PREPARATION The console should be displaying the main command line.

LEARNING ACTIVITY You have run programs two different ways with your computer. Most frequently, you have done this with the R(un command, which runs SYSTEM.WRK.CODE. A parallel function is available with the Execute command, which can run any .CODE file except SYSTEM.WRK.CODE. This was the command you used when you eX(ecuted DISKFORMAT.CODE to format your blank diskette. You can also use this command to execute a program you write.

1. Type **X** for X(ecute

```
Execute what file?
```

2. Type **TWINKLE** and press **Enter**.

```
Command: E(dit, R(un, F(ile, C(omp, X(ecute, U(ser restart [ED 1R0.0]
Twinkle, twinkle, little star.
How I wonder what you are.
Up above the world so high
Like a diamond in the sky.
```

The p-System can only execute .CODE files so it is not necessary to type the ending ".CODE" after the program name. If you do type the ".CODE" ending, the system will respond with an "Illegal file name" error message.

The Demo Program Included on your diskette is a p-System demonstration program which demonstrates many of the features you have learned so far, and shows you a few new tricks.

1. Type **X**.

```
Execute what file?
```

2. Type **SHOWDEMO** and press **Enter**.

3. Follow the instructions on the computer screen.

NOTE

If you need to make additional room on your diskette at some time, the files needed for the demonstration program can be either erased or transferred to your BLANK: diskette. The other files which can be eliminated are: SHOWDEMO.CODE, SCRIPT.TEXT, and DEMO.CODE.

WHAT YOU HAVE LEARNED

- Executing programs

REVIEW

1. The Execute command can run which files?

2. Which file will the Execute command not run?

3. When you are compiling a file other than SYSTEM.WRK.TEXT, what character causes the .CODE file to have the same name as the .TEXT file?

4. What computer language other than Pascal is available for the p-System?

PART 8
PROGRAMMING TECHNIQUES

WHAT YOU WILL LEARN

- Program structure
- Create a procedure
- Call a procedure
- Specify variable names
- Declare constants
- Assignment statement
- USES statement
- IBMSPECIAL unit
- NOTE procedure

Module 13
PROCEDURES AND PROGRAM STRUCTURE

KEY TOPICS

- Program structure
- Create a procedure
- Call a procedure

PRACTICE SESSION

Now you are ready to learn some of the basic syntax rules for programs and procedures.

PREPARATION

1. Use the **K**(runch Filer command to crunch your diskette.

2. Type **G** for G(et.

```
Get what file?
```

3. Type **TWINKLE** and press **Enter**

```
Get what file?
Text & Code file loaded
```

The G(et command has assigned file "TWINKLE.TEXT" as the file for the Editor to work with instead of SYSTEM.WRK.TEXT.

4. Quit the Filer.

LEARNING ACTIVITY The use of procedures allows you to add structure to your programs. This makes the programs easier to write and easier to read.

Program Structure A major advantage of the Pascal language over more primitive languages like BASIC is the ability to add structure to programs through the use of procedures. Procedures provide a way for you to extend the Pascal language to fit your special needs.

1. Type **E** for Edit and recall your program to the screen.

```
>Edit: A(djust C(opy D(el F(ind I(nsert J(ump K(ol M(argin P(age ? [ED 1R0.0]
{$Q+}
PROGRAM TWINKLE
BEGIN
    WRITELN ('Twinkle, twinkle, little star.');
    WRITELN ('How I wonder what you are.');
    WRITE ('Up ');
    WRITE ('above ');
    WRITE ('the');
    WRITE (' world ');
    WRITELN ('so high,');
    WRITELN ('Like a diamond in the sky.');
END.
```

The program as written prints only the first four lines of the poem. There are two ways of extending the program to print the remainder of the poem. You could add the lines:

```
WRITELN   ('Twinkle, twinkle, little star');
WRITELN   ('How I wonder what you are.');
```

at the end of the program steps, but that would involve repeating work already done.

What is needed is a way to use the lines of program text already written. The PROCEDURE is the way to do this!

Create a Procedure You have already encountered two of Pascal's built-in procedures, WRITE and WRITELN. Pascal allows you to create additional procedures as you build your program. A procedure is like a miniature program that fits inside your program.

1. Modify your program to look like the following one:

```
>Edit: A(djust C(opy D(el F(ind I(nsert J(ump K(ol M(argin P(age ? [ED 1R0.0]
PROGRAM TWINKLE;

PROCEDURE FIRSTWO;
BEGIN
    WRITELN ('Twinkle, twinkle, little star');
    WRITELN ('How I wonder what you are.');
End;

PROCEDURE MIDDLE;
BEGIN
    WRITE ('Up ');
    WRITE ('above ');
    WRITE ('the');
    WRITE (' world ');
    WRITELN ('so high');
    WRITELN ('Like a diamond in the sky');
END;

BEGIN
END.
```

Check your work for some common errors:

a. Are the END statements of each procedure followed by a semicolon?

b. Is the final END statement of the program followed by a period?

c. Did you remove the quiet compile switch?

2. Compile the program.

```
Command:  E(dit,  R(un,  F(ile,  C(omp,  X(ecute,  U(ser restart [ED 1R0.0]
Output file for compiled listing? (<cr> for none)

Pascal compiler - release level [ED 1R0.0-2]
<    0>....
FIRSTWO
<    4>......
MIDDLE
<   10>.........
TWINKLE
<   19>...

TWINKLE  ...
```

The compiler status screen is longer this time. It identifies the name of each procedure as it compiles.

3. Type **R** to run the program.

```
Command:  E(dit,  R(un,  F(ile,  C(omp,  X(ecute,  U(ser restart [ED 1R0.0]
Running...
```

The program ran, but nothing happened. This program has defined all the procedures, but has not called any of them.

Calling Procedures The procedures FIRSTWO and MIDDLE are referred to by name. The "main program" is now an empty BEGIN-END group.

1. Type **E** for Edit.

2. Add three statements to the program as shown:

```
>Edit: A(djust C(opy D(el F(ind I(nsert J(ump K(ol M(argin P(age ? [ED 1R0.0]
PROGRAM TWINKLE;

PROCEDURE FIRSTWO;
BEGIN
    WRITELN ('Twinkle, twinkle, little star');
    WRITELN ('How I wonder what you are.');
End;

PROCEDURE MIDDLE;
BEGIN
    WRITE ('Up ');
    WRITE ('above ');
    WRITE ('the');
    WRITE (' world ');
    WRITELN ('so high');
    WRITELN ('Like a diamond in the sky');
END;

BEGIN
    FIRSTWO;
    MIDDLE;
    FIRSTWO;
END.
```

3. Run the program.

```
Command: E(dit, R(un, F(ile, C(omp, X(ecute, U(ser restart [ED 1R0.0]
Running...
Twinkle, twinkle, little star.
How I wonder what you are.
Up above the world so high
Like a diamond in the sky.
Twinkle, twinkle, little star.
How I wonder what you are.
```

The complete poem appears on the screen.

WHAT YOU HAVE LEARNED

- Program structure
- Create a procedure
- Call a procedure

REVIEW

1. What is an advantage of PASCAL over more primitive languages?

2. What is a PASCAL procedure?

3. List two reasons procedures are useful.

Module 14
VARIABLES AND CONSTANTS

KEY TOPICS

- Specify variable names
- Assignment Statement
- Declare constants

PRACTICE SESSION

One of the real advantages of computer programs is the ability of the programmer to designate certain variables in the program and have the computer manipulate them to produce specified output.

PREPARATION No preparation is required for this module.

LEARNING ACTIVITY The computer programs you have written so far have produced literal output on the screen. There was no reason for anything in the program to have a different value. To perform tasks more complex than printing poetry on the screen, you need additional tools with which to work. One powerful tool is the use of variables.

A variable is a location in the computer memory used to store information. This location has much in common with a mailbox. The computer program can place information in the location, and change that information. The computer needs to know two things about these locations (mailboxes) to create and use them. First, the computer must have a name for the location, and second, the computer must know what kind of information the location must contain. Just as mailboxes must be different sizes to accommodate letters and packages, variable locations must be different sizes to accommodate different types of data.

A constant is similar to a variable in that it allows you to give a name to a value used in a program. The difference between a constant and a variable is that a constant can have only one value in a program. In a program performing calculations on circles, it would be useful to declare PI as 3.14159.

Names for Variables and Constants Just as the p-System has rules for filenames, the Pascal compiler has rules for identifiers of variables and constants:

- Names must start with a letter (A-Z).
- All other characters in the identifier must be letters (A-Z), numbers (0-9), or an underscore(_). The underscore is ignored by the Pascal compiler.
- There is no limit on the length of an identifier, but UCSD Pascal only pays attention to the first eight characters.
- Identifiers must not be the same as a Pascal reserved word. (See Appendix B for a list of reserved words.)

Because the underscore character is ignored in variable names, TOTAL_PAY is the same variable as TOTALPAY.

Pascal does not differentiate between uppercase and lowercase characters in identifiers. The following variable names are all identical: TOTAL, total, Total, ToTaL.

Examples of valid identifiers include: COST, SUM, PAYRATE, TOTAL, SUM1, K3425, THIS _IS_A_LONG_ VARIABLE_NAME.

Examples of invalid identifiers include:

4THQUARTER	(starts with a number)
PAY#24	(includes a special character)
WRITE	(Pascal reserved word)
TOTAL PAY	(includes a space)

Because UCSD Pascal only looks at the first eight characters of the name, the compiler cannot tell the variables INCOME_TAX_FEDERAL and INCOME_TAX_STATE apart. To specify long variable names, make sure that they contain a difference within the first eight characters. The compiler would treat STATE_INCOME_TAX and FEDERAL_INCOME_TAX as separate variables.

The Assignment Statement Now that you know how to name a variable, let's look at the method of placing data in the variable's location. This task is accomplished with the assignment statement. The symbol := is used as the assignment operator in Pascal. It is composed of two characters, a colon and an equal sign. Assignment statements could look like:

```
PAY:=135.23;
TAX:=89.21;
```

The first statement takes the number 135.23 and places it in location PAY. The second statement takes the number 89.21 and places it in TAX.

It is also possible to place the value of one variable in the location of another variable. For example

```
PAY:=135.23;
TAX:=PAY;
```

would place the number 135.23 in location PAY, then would take the contents of location PAY (which happens to be 135.23) and place it in TAX. When both statements have been executed, PAY and TAX both contain the value 135.23.

Do not confuse the symbols for assignment, :=, and equality, =. The statement

```
COUNT = COUNT + 1
```

is a statement of mathematical equality that can never be true. The statement

```
COUNT := COUNT + 1;
```

is a valid and extremely useful assignment statement. It means:

- Take the number stored in location COUNT.
- Add 1 to the number.
- Place the result in COUNT.

Assignment and equality are two completely different concepts.

Declaring Constants Constants are declared and given a value in a CONST statement. The CONST statement follows immediately after the PROGRAM statement.

To declare PI as 3.14159 you would write:

```
PROGRAM CIRCLES;

CONST PI=3.14159;

{Other program statements}

BEGIN

{Other program statements}

END.
```

The constant declaration is different from a variable assignment. Notice that the = sign is used instead of the assignment symbol. This is because you are making a statement of equality, not assigning a value to a variable.

WHAT YOU HAVE LEARNED

- Specify variable names
- Assignment statements
- Declare constants

REVIEW

1. What is a variable?

2. What does the computer need to know to create a variable?

3. What characters can be used in a variable name?

4. The Compiler only reads how many characters of a variable name?

5. What symbol assigns a value to a variable?

6. What symbol associates a value with a constant?

Module 15
MAKING MUSIC

KEY TOPICS

- USES Statement
- NOTE procedure

PRACTICE SESSION

The IBM PC family of computers has a number of features not found on all computers and not directly accessable through Pascal.

You have seen how procedures can be used to give a program structure. Procedures can also be used to add features not found in the Pascal language. A number of procedures for taking advantage of the special features of the IBM PC family have been written for you and placed in SYSTEM.LIBRARY on your STUDENT: diskette.

PREPARATION Enter the Editor, recalling program TWINKLE to the screen.

LEARNING ACTIVITY The first step in making music is to add a statement to your program to tell the compiler to access the unit of procedures called IBMSPECIAL. This is done with a USES statement. The USES statement must be located before using any of the procedures in the unit.

1. Add the USES statement immediately after the PROGRAM statement.

   PROGRAM TWINKLE;
   USES IBMSPECIAL;

The procedure you use for working with music is:

NOTE(pitch, octave, duration);

The value of "pitch" is a number from 0 through 12 interpreted as follows:

0	Rest	1 C	7 F#
		2 C#	8 G
		3 D	9 G#
		4 D#	10 A
		5 E	11 A#
		6 F	12 B

The values for "octave" range from 0 to 7; octave 0 is the lowest octave and octave 7 the highest.

"Duration" is measured in milliseconds. (There are 1000 milliseconds in a second.)

Since you have a program which prints "Twinkle, Twinkle, Little Star" on the screen, it would be nice to play the music along with the words. The music is:

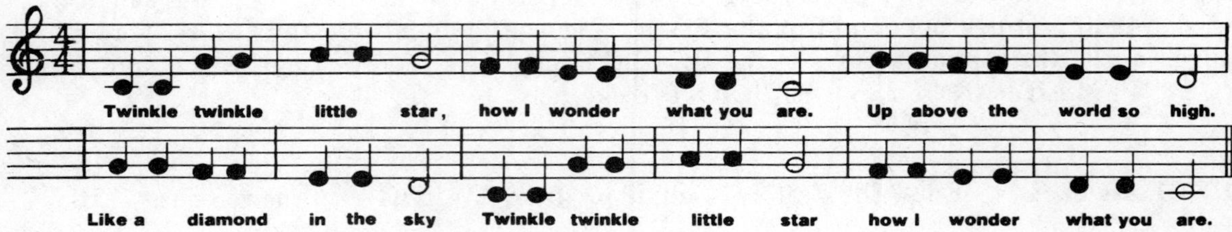

Although the poem has six lines, there are only three different musical patterns used for the music. The last three lines are a repeat of the first three, but in a different order. The notes needed in the song are C, D, E, F, G and A.

Instead of referencing the values for "pitch", "octave", and "duration" by number throughout the procedures you develop; assign them to constants. That way, the procedures are both more readable and more easily modified.

2. Immediately after the USES statement, add a constant declaration as follows:

```
PROGRAM TWINKLE;
USES IBMSPECIAL;
CONST REST=0; C=1; D=3; E=5; F=6; G=8; A=10;
```

There are two lengths of notes used in the song, quarter notes, and half notes. A length of 300 for quarter notes and 600 for half notes gives a good starting point. Octave 3 is a good starting point for the octave.

3. Add values for QUARTER, HALF, and OCTAVE to the constant declaration.

Pascal requires a procedure be declared before it is used. Because there are three unique lines of music, create three procedures. Make them the first three procedures in the program. Name them LINE1, LINE2, and LINE3.

4. Add procedure LINE1 as shown:

```
PROCEDURE LINE1;
BEGIN
          NOTE(C,OCTAVE,QUARTER);
          NOTE(C,OCTAVE,QUARTER);
          NOTE(G,OCTAVE,QUARTER);
          NOTE(G,OCTAVE,QUARTER);
          NOTE(A,OCTAVE,QUARTER);
          NOTE(A,OCTAVE,QUARTER);
          NOTE(G,OCTAVE,HALF);
END;
```

5. Write and add procedure LINE2. The notes needed are FFEEDDC. All but the last note are quarter notes.

6. Write and add procedure LINE3. The notes needed are GGFFEED. All but the last note are quarter notes.

Good programming structure dictates that the main program be kept as simple as possible. Therefore, instead of calling the music procedures from the main program, call them from the procedures that print the lines of text. Use the strategy of first writing a single line on the screen, then playing the music.

7. Modify procedure FIRSTWO as follows:

```
PROCEDURE FIRSTWO;
BEGIN
        WRITELN('Twinkle, twinkle, little star.');
        LINE1;
        WRITELN('How I wonder what you are.');
        LINE2
END;
```

8. Modify procedure MIDDLE by calling LINE3 twice.

9. Run the program.

The music is recognizable, but when two notes having the same pitch are played right after each other they seem to run together. The effect can be improved by inserting a short pause or rest between the notes.

10. Insert the statement **NOTE(REST,0,20);** between each of the existing NOTE statements. HINT: Use the C(opy B(uffer Editor procedure to save typing effort.

11. Run the program.

The individual notes are now more distinct. By varying the length of the rest between the notes you can change the musical style from staccato to legato.

Good Programming Technique Pays Off Using good programming style sometimes seems like extra effort when writing a program. It pays off in the long run.

Problem: Play the song twice as fast. Solution: If you had used statements like:

```
NOTE(1,3,300);
```

to play the music this problem would involve changing a large number of program statements. Because you used good structure and declared QUARTER and HALF as constants, you only need to change two values.

1. Change the value of QUARTER to 150 and HALF to 300.

2. Run the program.

Always strive to make your programs as well structured and flexible as possible. You never know how you may later want to modify your code for a different application. The benefits in the long run are well worth the effort.

WHAT YOU HAVE LEARNED

- USES statement
- NOTE procedure

REVIEW

1. Write the statement that allows the compiler to access the procedures in the IBM SPECIAL unit.

2. What is the advantage of using constants or variables instead of numbers?

3. How could you change the program to play the song an octave higher?

PART 9
ASSIGNMENT STATEMENT

WHAT YOU WILL LEARN

- VAR statement
- Declaration of INTEGER variables
- Assignment of INTEGER variables
- INTEGER output
- Range of INTEGER variables
- Declaration of REAL variables
- Assignment of REAL variables
- REAL output
- Range of REAL variables
- Numeric precision of REAL variables

Module 16
INTEGER VARIABLE ASSIGNMENT

KEY TOPICS

- VAR statement
- Declaration of INTEGER variables
- Assignment of INTEGER variables
- INTEGER output
- Range of INTEGER variables

PRACTICE SESSION One of the built-in types of variables Pascal has available is the INTEGER. Integers are the whole number — positive, negative and zero. In mathematics, the set of integers consists of {...,–3,–2,–1, 0, 1, 2, 3, ...}.

PREPARATION Crunch your diskette to consolidate the unused space. Use the N(ew command to clear the workfile. Return to the main command level.

LEARNING ACTIVITY The internal representation of integers in the computer's memory provides both benefits and limitations. Integer arithmetic is very fast. The computer can manipulate whole numbers much faster than it can decimals. The computer also uses less storage for integers than decimals. These benefits come at a price. The set of integers in Pascal does not extend infinitely in both directions. There is both a smallest and a largest integer provided by the computer.

Range of Integers The largest and smallest integers available in Pascal vary from one computer to another. UCSD Pascal is designed to be as portable as possible, and not dependent on the hardware characteristics of any particular computer. As a result, there is no fixed minimum and maximum integer established by Pascal for the size of integers.

Pascal provides a constant, MAXINT, which is automatically set equal to the largest integer available on the computer. The range of integers extends from a maximum of MAXINT to a minimum of negative MAXINT. In the IBM PC family of computers, MAXINT, the largest integer, is 32767, making integers {–32767...–1, 0, 1,...32767}. Use MAXINT in your programs instead of 32767 whenever you need the largest integer.

VAR Statement Pascal requires all variables to be declared. This is done with the VAR statement. The VAR statement requires you to list each variable you use in the program and specify the variable's type.

1. Type **E** to enter the Editor and create a new file.

2. Give the program the name ASSIGN.

```
>Insert: Text {<bs> a char, <del> a line} [<ext> accepts, <esc> escapes]
PROGRAM ASSIGN;
```

The VAR statement goes after the CONST statement, or the PROGRAM statement if there is no CONST statement, and before the first PROCEDURE statement or the main program BEGIN statement. Some convenient names for integer variables are I ,J, K and L. Any valid name would work, but programmers traditionally use these as integer variables. The first step in using integer variables is to declare them in the VAR statement.

3. Add the statement: **VAR I,J,K,L : INTEGER;**

```
>Insert: Text {<bs> a char, <del> a line} [<ext> accepts, <esc> escapes]
PROGRAM ASSIGN;

VAR I,J,K,L : INTEGER;
```

This statement tells the compiler to reserve space for four integers I, J, K and L. It does not place any value in the locations. A common mistake among beginning Pascal programmers is assuming the compiler will assign 0 to all variables. The values stored in the locations I, J, K, and L consist of whatever numbers have been stored in these memory locations previously.

Now that the locations have been reserved, assign some values to these variables with the assignment statement.

4. Add the following statements to the program:

```
>Insert: Text {<bs> a char, <del> a line} [<ext> accepts, <esc> escapes]
PROGRAM ASSIGN;

VAR I,J,K,L : INTEGER;

BEGIN
    I:=12;
    J:=-892;
    K:=MAXINT;
    L:=-32767;
END.
```

5. Run the program.

```
Command: E(dit, R(un, F(ile, C(omp, X(ecute, U(ser restart [ED 1R0.0]
Running...
```

The computer has carried out your instructions but has not shared its work with you. Output statements are needed to tell the computer you want it to share the values of the variables with you.

6. Add a WRITELN statement as shown:

```
>Insert: Text {<bs> a char, <del> a line} [<ext> accepts, <esc> escapes]
PROGRAM ASSIGN;

VAR I,J,K,L : INTEGER;

BEGIN
    I:=12;
    J:=-892;
    K:=MAXINT;
    L:=-32767;
    WRITELN(I,J,K,L);
END.
```

7. Run the program.

WHAT YOU HAVE LEARNED

- VAR statement
- Declaration of INTEGER variables
- Assignment of INTEGER variables
- INTEGER output
- Range of INTEGER variables

REVIEW

1. What is the value of MAXINT in the IBM PC family of computers?

2. What is the purpose of the VAR statement?

3. Where does the VAR statement go in the program?

4. What is a limitation, other than MAXINT, on INTEGER values?

5. What is an advantage of INTEGER variables?

Module 17
REAL VARIABLES

KEY TOPICS

- Declaration of REAL variables
- Assignment of REAL variables
- REAL variable output
- Range of REAL variables
- Numeric precision of REAL variables

PRACTICE SESSION

REAL variables are a second built-in variable type in Pascal. A real number is any number which can be expressed as an integer and any number of decimal digits.

PREPARATION Crunch your diskette to consolidate the unused space. Use the N(ew command to clear the workfile. Return to the main command level.

LEARNING ACTIVITY The internal representation of real numbers in the computer's memory provides both benefits and limitations. Integers were limited, on the IBM PC, to the range — 32767 to 32767. Real numbers can be considerably larger and smaller. Real numbers, however, are less accurate and require more computer time to perform computations.

Range of REAL Variables The IBM PC APPRENTICE version of the p-System stores REAL numbers in a memory space equal to two integers. They can range in value from 1.0E–38 to 1.0E+38. The limitations of real numbers include having only five digits of accuracy and requiring significantly more time for the computer to perform mathematical computations. REAL variables also occupy twice as much memory as integers, which may be a limitation for some applications.

NOTE

The full version of the p-System has provision for storing REAL variables in a memory space equal to four integers. These can range from 1.0E–308 to 1.0E+308 with 16 digits of precision.

Declaration of REAL Variables REAL variables are declared in the same VAR statement as INTEGERS. Each REAL variable must be listed together with the designator REAL.

1. Type **E** to enter the Editor and create a new file.

2. Give the program the name REALS.

```
>Insert: Text {<bs> a char, <del> a line} [<ext> accepts, <esc> escapes]
PROGRAM REALS;
```

The VAR statement is the same VAR statement used for declaring INTEGER variables. To illustrate this point, let's have both INTEGER and REAL variables in this program.

3. Add the VAR statement as shown:

```
>Insert: Text {<bs> a char, <del> a line} [<ext> accepts, <esc> escapes]
PROGRAM REALS;

VAR I,J : INTEGER;
    X,Y : REAL;
```

This variable declaration has reserved space for four variables. **I** and **J** are INTEGERS, **X** and **Y** are REAL.

Let's assign some values to these variables.

4. Assign **I** to be 325
   J to be 71
   X to be 87.3
   Y to be 19823.9788923

5. Use the WRITELN statement to display the values on the screen.

```
>Insert: Text {<bs> a char, <del> a line} [<ext> accepts, <esc> escapes]
PROGRAM REALS;

VAR I,J : INTEGER;
    X,Y : REAL;

BEGIN
    I:=325;
    J:=71;
    X:=87.3;
    Y:=19823.9788923;
    WRITELN(I,' ',J,X,Y);
END.
```

6. Run the program.

```
Command: E(dit, R(un, F(ile, C(omp, X(ecute, U(ser restart [ED 1R0.0]
Running...
325 71 8.73000E1 1.98240E4
```

The output line may appear somewhat strange if you are not used to reading scientific or exponential notation. Unless you specify otherwise, REAL numbers are printed in exponential notation. 8.73000E1 is 8.73000 * 10^1, which is 87.3000. 1.98240E4 is 1.98240 * 10^4, which is 19824.0. Notice that the number you got out is not the same as the number you put in. This is because you have attemped to exceed the precision of the computer's representation of real numbers.

WHAT YOU HAVE LEARNED

- Declaration of REAL variables
- Assignment of REAL variables
- REAL variable output
- Range of REAL variables
- Numeric precision of REAL variables

REVIEW

1. What is the range of REAL variables?

2. Unless otherwise specified REAL variables are output in what format?

3. How many digits of accuracy are available for REAL values in the Pascal compiler?

4. What is an advantage of a REAL variable over an INTEGER variable?

5. What is a disadvantage of a REAL variable compared to an INTEGER variable?

PART 10
CHARACTER VARIABLES AND TYPE MATCHING

WHAT YOU WILL LEARN

- Declaration of character variables
- Assignment of character variables
- Character variable output
- Length of STRING variables
- Type mismatch errors
- Automatic type conversions

Module 18
CHARACTER VARIABLES

KEY TOPICS

- Declaration of character variables
- Assignment of character variables
- Character variable output
- Length of STRING variables

PRACTICE SESSION

Numeric variables are not the only types available. Characters and groups of characters can also be assigned to variables.

PREPARATION Use the N(ew command to clear the workfile. Q(uit the Filer and return to the main Command line.

LEARNING ACTIVITY There are two ways of storing character information in Pascal. Single characters can be stored in a variable type called CHAR. Groups of characters comprising words, sentences, and phrases can be stored in the variable type STRING.

Declaration of Character Variables Single characters may be assigned to a variable of type CHAR. However, English is not often treated as single characters, but rather as groups of characters; words, phrases, and sentences are more natural. UCSD Pascal provides a variable type of STRING to handle groups of characters. A string is different from other variable types in that it does not have a fixed length in memory. The length of a string can change during the execution of a program. The Pascal compiler needs to know in advance the maximum length of a string. If you do not tell the compiler this information, it will provide a maximum length of 80 characters. You can specify any length from 0 to 255 as the maximum length. (A STRING of length 0 would not be especially useful, but the compiler will let you specify it if you want.)

1. Type **E** to enter the editor and press **Enter** to create a new file.

2. Create a program named CHARACTERS.

```
>Insert: Text {<bs> a char, <del> a line} [<ext> accepts, <esc> escapes]
PROGRAM CHARACTERS;
```

The maximum length of a string is specified by enclosing the number of characters in brackets. You can declare strings of different lengths in the same program.

3. Declare INPUT as a variable of type CHAR, NAME and ADDRESS to be STRINGs of maximum length 30 and STATE to be a string of maximum length 2.

```
>Insert: Text {<bs> a char, <del> a line} [<ext> accepts, <esc> escapes]
PROGRAM CHARACTERS;

VAR INPUT:CHAR;
    NAME, ADDRESS:STRING[30];
    STATE:STRING[2];
```

Assignment of Characters You have had some experience with strings of characters in Pascal. Pascal allows you to specify literal characters by enclosing them in single quotation marks. Use this technique to assign values to the variables in this example.

1. Assign **Y** to INPUT
   Jane Smith to NAME
   1828 Disk Drive to ADDRESS
   TX to STATE.

```
>Edit: A(djust C(opy D(el F(ind I(nsert J(ump K(ol M(argin P(age ? [ED 1R0.0]
PROGRAM CHARACTERS;

VAR INPUT:CHAR;
    NAME, ADDRESS:STRING[30];
    STATE:STRING[2];

BEGIN
    INPUT:='Y';
    NAME:='Jane Smith';
    ADDRESS:='1828 Disk Drive';
    STATE:='TX';
```

You won't be able to see this work without some output statements, so add some WRITELN statements to display the value of the variables.

2. Add WRITELN statements to display the variable values.

```
>Edit: A(djust C(opy D(el F(ind I(nsert J(ump K(ol M(argin P(age ? [ED 1R0.0]
PROGRAM CHARACTERS;

VAR INPUT:CHAR;
    NAME, ADDRESS:STRING[30];
    STATE:STRING[2];

BEGIN
    INPUT:='Y';
    NAME:='Jane Smith';
    ADDRESS:='1828 Disk Drive';
    STATE:='TX';
    WRITELN(INPUT);
    WRITELN(NAME);
    WRITELN(ADDRESS);
    WRITELN(STATE);
END.
```

3. Run the program.

```
Command: E(dit, R(un, F(ile, C(omp, X(ecute, U(ser restart [ED 1R0.0]
Running...
Y
Jane Smith
1828 Disk Drive
TX
```

WHAT YOU HAVE LEARNED

- Declaration of character variables
- Assignment of character variables
- Character variable output
- Length of STRING variables

REVIEW

1. How is a variable STRING different from other variables?

2. If a variable STRING isn't assigned a length how long will the computer make it?

3. How long can a variable STRING be?

4. What happens when characters are enclosed in quotation marks?

5. How short can a STRING be?

Module 19
TYPE MATCHING

KEY TOPICS

- Character variables
- Numeric literals

PRACTICE SESSION

Some of the most common errors in program development occur when the programmer attempts to mix variable types.

PREPARATION The computer console should show the main command line.

LEARNING ACTIVITY When computer scientists classify computer languages, one of the descriptions applied to the Pascal language is that Pascal is a "strongly typed language." This does not mean that the programmer must hit the keys forcefully when typing the program. It means, instead, that except for a few rigidly defined exceptions, variables of one "type" can not be assigned to variables of another type with an assignment statement.

1. Enter the Editor and call up the program from the previous module.

```
>Edit: A(djust C(opy D(el F(ind I(nsert J(ump K(ol M(argin P(age ? [ED 1R0.0]
PROGRAM CHARACTERS;

VAR INPUT:CHAR;
    NAME, ADDRESS:STRING[30];
    STATE:STRING[2];

BEGIN
    INPUT:='Y';
    NAME:='Jane Smith';
    ADDRESS:='1828 Disk Drive';
    STATE:='TX';
    WRITELN(INPUT);
    WRITELN(NAME);
    WRITELN(ADDRESS);
    WRITELN(STATE);
END.
```

2. Change “STATE:='TX';” to “STATE:=INPUT;” to assign the character “Y” to the string STATE.

3. Compile the program.

```
Compiling...
```

The compiler has found a type mismatch error. It seems reasonable that you should be able to assign a CHAR variable to a STRING, as both contain characters, but such is not the case. A CHAR cannot be assigned to a STRING, and a STRING cannot be assigned to a CHAR; this is true even if the declaration for the string is STRING[1].

Numeric Literals Pascal also makes assumptions about the numbers assigned to INTEGER and REAL variables.

1. Use the G(et Filer command to assign REALS as the current workfile.

2. Exit the Filer and enter the Editor.

Your program appears on the screen:

```
>Edit: A(djust C(opy D(el F(ind I(nsert J(ump K(ol M(argin P(age ? [ED 1R0.0]
PROGRAM REALS;

VAR I,J : INTEGER;
    X,Y : REAL;

BEGIN
    I:=325;
    J:=71;
    X:=87.3;
    Y:=19823.9788923;
    WRITELN(I,' ',J,X,Y);
END.
```

3. Change the assignment statement for I to **I:=325.0**.

4. Change the assignment statement for X to **X:=87**.

5. **Q**(uit the Editor, **U**(pdate the workfile, **C**(compile the program, press **Enter**.

```
Compiling...
Output file for compiled listing? (<cr> for none)

Pascal compiler - release level [ED 1R0.0-2]
<    0>......
REALS
<    6>
    BEGIN
        I:=325.0; <---
Type conflict of operands
Line 7
Type <sp> to continue, <esc> to terminate, or 'e' to edit_
```

The compiler has identified 325.0 as a REAL number because it contains a decimal point. Type matching does not allow the assignment of a REAL number to an INTEGER variable.

6. Press the **Spacebar** to continue.

```
Compiling...
Output file for compiled listing? (<cr> for none)

Pascal compiler - release level [ED 1R0.0-2]
<    0>......
REALS
<    6>
    BEGIN
       I:=325.0; <---
Type conflict of operands
Line 7
Type <sp> to continue, <esc> to terminate, or 'e' to edit
<    6>..
       J:=71;
       X:=87. <---
Error in real number - digit expected
Line 9
Type <sp> to continue, <esc> to terminate, or 'e' to edit_
```

A REAL number specification must contain a decimal point, and the decimal point must be followed by a digit. If not, the compiler will flag it as an error.

7. Press **Esc** to terminate the compilation.

The compiler assumes that any number with a decimal point is REAL and any number without one is INTEGER. Even though the assignments are assigning whole numbers to INTEGER variables, the compiler objects because of the decimal point. Whole numbers are also perfectly good REAL numbers, but without the decimal point, the compiler objects.

These assignments must be rewritten as:

```
I:= 325;
X:= 87.0;
```

Type checking may seem like an unnecessary burden, especially if you have previously programmed in a language without strong type checking. Strong typing, however, helps prevent you from making errors that are extremely hard to track down. Pascal is designed to assist you in creating error-free programs, and strong typing is one of the ways it does this.

WHAT YOU HAVE LEARNED

- Character variables
- Numeric literals

REVIEW

1. What is meant when a programming language is defined as "strongly typed"?

2. What is a characteristic of a REAL variable that distinguishes it from an INTEGER variable?

PART 11
ARITHMETIC AND NUMERIC OUTPUT

WHAT YOU WILL LEARN

- Arithmetic operators
- Arithmetic precedence
- Alter natural precedence
- Create WRITE parameter list
- Default INTEGER formatting
- Default REAL formatting
- Adjust column width
- Adjust decimal position

Module 20
ARITHMETIC

KEY TOPICS

- Arithmetic operators
- Arithmetic precedence
- Alter natural precedence

PRACTICE SESSION

In order to accurately manipulate numerical variables it is important that you understand some basic rules of operation.

PREPARATION Enter the Filer from the main command line. Set the system date and clear the workfile.

LEARNING ACTIVITY The use of arithmetic is a fundamental part of computer programming. Pascal provides for the standard arithmetic operations of addition, subtraction, multiplication, and two types of division, integer division and real division.

Operand Types INTEGER variables and REAL variables have different operations that are performed on them. Because different types of numeric values are stored differently in memory, the computer must have separate operations for each. Even though the only visible difference in the symbols is in the division operations, there is a difference between INTEGER arithmetic and REAL arithmetic from the computer's point of view.

Every arithmetic assignment statement has a "type" of either REAL or INTEGER. The type of the destination variable determines the type of arithmetic used.

Integer Operators Although the arithmetic operations are those you are familiar with from the study of mathematics, Pascal has different notations for some of these to prevent confusion between symbols. The symbols for INTEGER operations are:

*	Multiplication
DIV	Division
MOD	Remainder
+	Addition
–	Subtraction

There are several differences you can see between this list and the list of operators used in mathematics. Multiplication is designated by * instead of **x** or **X** to prevent the multiplication operation from becoming confused with a variable named "X." There are two operations associated with division, the DIV operation and the MOD operation. The DIV operation computes the quotient of two integers, ignoring the remainder. The MOD operation computes the remainder of the division operation, ignoring the quotient.

An INTEGER assignment statement may only contain INTEGER constants and INTEGER variables combined with INTEGER operations.

Real Operators The symbols for REAL operations are:

*	Multiplication
/	Division
+	Addition
–	Subtraction

A REAL assignment statement may only contain REAL constants, REAL variables, INTEGER constants, INTEGER variables, and REAL operations. The computer converts the INTEGER variables to REAL quantities as it performs the operation.

Arithmetic Assignment Assuming that the variables have been properly declared as REAL or INTEGER, the following examples show possible arithmetic assignment statements.

```
SUM:=X+Y+Z;
GRPAY:=HOURS * RATE;
NET:=GRPAY - TAX;
DISTANCE:=VELOCITY * TIME;
AREA:=3.14159 * RADIUS * RADIUS;
```

1. Enter the Editor and create a program called MATH.

2. Declare the variables X,Y, and Z to be REAL.

3. Declare the variables I,J, and K to be INTEGER.

```
>Insert: Text {<bs> a char, <del> a line} [<ext> accepts, <esc> escapes]
PROGRAM MATH;

VAR X, Y, Z : REAL;
    I, J, K : INTEGER;
```

4. Add the following assignment statements:

```
I:=2+3;
J:=27350  -  21845;
K:=I  *  2  +  1;
X:=2/3;
Y:=3.14159  *  5  *  5;
Z:=  X  +  Y;
```

5. Add WRITELN statements to label the values and print them.

```
>Insert: Text {<bs> a char, <del> a line} [<ext> accepts, <esc> escapes]
PROGRAM MATH;

VAR X, Y, Z : REAL;
    I, J, K : INTEGER;

BEGIN
    I:=2+3;
    J:=27350 - 21845;
    K:=I * 2 + 1;
    X:=2/3;
    Y:=3.14159 * 5 * 5;
    Z:= X + Y;
    WRITELN('The value of I is: ',I);
    WRITELN('The value of J is: ',J);
    WRITELN('The value of K is: ',K);
    WRITELN('The value of X is: ',X);
    WRITELN('The value of Y is: ',Y);
    WRITELN('The value of Z is: ',Z);
END.
```

6. Run the program.

```
Command:  E(dit,  R(un, F(ile, C(omp, X(ecute, U(ser restart [ED 1R0.0]
Running...
The value of I is: 5
The value of J is: 5505
The value of K is: 11
The value of X is: 6.66667E-1
The value of Y is: 7.85397E1
The value of Z is: 7.92064E1
```

The computer appears to have provided the correct answers.

Arithmetic Precedence The meaning of arithmetic assignment statements could be confusing if Pascal did not have rules for determining the order in which operations are performed. In the program you just finished, for example, the value of "K" was computed by first multiplying 5 (the value of "I") by 2 and then adding 1.

In Pascal, multiplication and division are performed before addition and subtraction. The order of operations within a level of precedence is undefined. The statement

```
X:= 45 + 23 * 4 - 10 / 2
```

is evaluated as follows: "23 * 4" and "10 / 2" are evaluated first, giving 92 because multiplication and division are performed before addition. It is not possible to determine whether the multiplication or division is performed first. This leaves 45 + 92 + 5. Addition and subtraction have the same precedence, so the order of operations is undefined. Because addition is commutative (subtraction is actually addition of signed numbers), 45 + 92 – 5 yields 132 regardless of the order in which the operations are performed. The number 132 is assigned to "X."

Following the rules of precedence is important! If these operations had been simply performed from left to right, ignoring the rules of precedence, the result would have been 131.

Altering Precedence Sometimes you may find it difficult to express a formula using the natural precedence provided by Pascal. Other times, the natural precedence may not be immediately apparent when you look at a formula. Parentheses may be used to change the order of operations, and to make formulas more readable. The previous example,

```
X:=45 + 23 * 4 - 10 / 2
```

could be rewritten as X:= 45 + (23 * 4) – (10 / 2).

The operation in the innermost parentheses is performed first. 45 + 23 = 68. The second level of parentheses directs that the next operation should be 68 * 4, giving 272. The outer level of parentheses dictates that the next operation is 272–10. This result, 262, is divided by 2 giving 131.

```
X:= (((45 + 23) * 4) - 10) / 2
```

The operation in the innermost parentheses is performed first. 45 + 23 = 68. The second level of parentheses directs that the next operation should be 68 * 4, giving 272. The outer level of parentheses dictate that the next operation is 272–10. This result, 262, is divided by 2 giving 131.

Even when the natural order of precedence provides the correct order of operations, it is good programming practice to clarify the operation with the use of parentheses.

1. Enter the Editor and delete the right hand side of all the assignment statements.

```
>Edit: A(djust C(opy D(el F(ind I(nsert J(ump K(ol M(argin P(age ? [ED 1R0.0]
PROGRAM MATH;

VAR X, Y, Z : REAL;
    I, J, K : INTEGER;


BEGIN
    I:=
    J:=
    K:=
    X:=
    Y:=
    Z:=
    WRITELN('The value of I is: ',I);
    WRITELN('The value of J is: ',J);
    WRITELN('The value of K is: ',K);
    WRITELN('The value of X is: ',X);
    WRITELN('The value of Y is: ',Y);
    WRITELN('The value of Z is: ',Z);
END.
```

2. Change the assignment statements to read:

```
I:=3925  +  87  -  2015 DIV 90  *  45  +  100;
J:=((((3925  +  87)  -  2015) DIV 90)  *  45)  +  100;
K:=I  +  J;
X:=3925.0  +  87.0  -  2015.0 / 90.0  *  45.0  +  100.0;
Y:=(((((3925.0  +  87.0)  -  2015.0)  /  90.0)  *  45.0)  +  100.0);
Z:=X  +  Y;
```

There are two sets of similar assignment statements. The INTEGER set uses the "DIV" operator to perform integer division instead of the "/." The order of operations for "J" and "Y" is identical. The additional pair of parentheses in the expression for "Y" does not change the order and could be eliminated. Parentheses can be placed anywhere in the expression to require the enclosed operation to be performed first.

All parentheses come in pairs. Every expression must have the same number of opening and closing parentheses.

3. Check your work to assure that you have the same number of opening and closing parentheses in each expression.

4. Run the program.

```
Command:  E(dit,  R(un,  F(ile,  C(omp,  X(ecute,  U(ser restart [ED 1R0.0]
Running...
The value of I is: 3122
The value of J is: 1090
The value of K is: 4212
The value of X is: 3.10450E3
The value of Y is: 1.09850E3
The value of Z is: 4.20300E3
```

Converting X, Y, and Z to decimal notation, the values are

X=3104.5
Y=1098.5
Z=4203.0

The differences between I and J and between X and Y are the result of changing the order of operations with parentheses. The differences between I and X, J and Y, and K and Z are the result of the differences between REAL and INTEGER variables and operations.

WHAT YOU HAVE LEARNED

- Arithmetic operators
- Arithmetic precedence
- Altering natural precedence

REVIEW

1. What is the symbol for multiplication of REAL variables?

2. What is the symbol for division of INTEGER variables?

3. How would you write 6 times 5.3 divided by 32?

4. Which mathematical operations are always performed first?

5. Which mathematical operations are always performed last?

6. How can the order of precedence of mathematical operations be altered?

7. Evaluate **1 + 3 * 5**

8. Evaluate **3 DIV 1 + 2**

9. Evaluate **(3 + 1) * 4**

10. Evaluate **4 DIV (6 - 2)**

Module 21
NUMERIC OUTPUT

KEY TOPICS

- Create WRITE parameter list
- Default INTEGER formatting
- Default REAL formatting
- Adjust column width
- Adjust decimal position

PRACTICE SESSION

Defining variables is only the beginning. You must be able to print the variables out if you are to correct errors and communicate the results to others.

PREPARATION The computer console should show the main command line.

LEARNING ACTIVITY The standard output format for numbers provided by Pascal is not always the most appropriate. When the appearance of the output is important, Pascal provides features for formatting your numbers to meet your specifications.

The Parameter List When specifying output, it is necessary to distinguish between the name of a variable and the value of a variable. For example, if COUNT is declared as an INTEGER variable and assigned the value 17, the statement "WRITE(COUNT);" produces as output "17." The statement "WRITE('COUNT');" produces the output COUNT. Anything enclosed in quotation marks is printed literally on the screen. Entries not enclosed in quotes are interpreted as variables and their value is printed.

Default Integer Formatting If you do not specify a format to print INTEGER values, the computer will print them using one space for each digit in the number.

1. Enter the Editor, recalling MATH to the screen.

```
>Edit: A(djust C(opy D(el F(ind I(nsert J(ump K(ol M(argin P(age ? [ED 1R0.0]
PROGRAM MATH;

VAR X, Y, Z : REAL;
    I, J, K : INTEGER;

BEGIN
    I:=3925 + 87 - 2015 DIV 90 * 45 + 100;
    J:=((((3925 + 87) - 2015) DIV 90) * 45) + 100;
    K:=I + J;
    X:=3925.0 + 87.0 - 2015.0 / 90.0 * 45.0 + 100.0;
    Y:=(((((3925.0 + 87.0) - 2015.0) / 90.0) * 45.0) + 100.0);
    Z:=X + Y;
    WRITELN('The value of I is: ',I);
    WRITELN('The value of J is: ',J);
    WRITELN('The value of K is: ',K);
    WRITELN('The value of X is: ',X);
    WRITELN('The value of Y is: ',Y);
    WRITELN('The value of Z is: ',Z);
END.
```

Modify the output to place the three integer values all on the same line.

2. Delete the WRITELN statements for I, J, and K.

3. Add the statements:

WRITE ('The values of I, J, and K are: ');
WRITELN (I, J, K);

```
>Edit: A(djust C(opy D(el F(ind I(nsert J(ump K(ol M(argin P(age ? [ED 1R0.0]
PROGRAM MATH;

VAR X, Y, Z : REAL;
    I, J, K : INTEGER;

BEGIN
    I:=3925 + 87 - 2015 DIV 90 * 45 + 100;
    J:=((((3925 + 87) - 2015) DIV 90) * 45) + 100;
    K:=I + J;
    X:=3925.0 + 87.0 - 2015.0 / 90.0 * 45.0 + 100.0;
    Y:=(((((3925.0 + 87.0) - 2015.0) / 90.0) * 45.0) + 100.0);
    Z:=X + Y;
    WRITE ('The values of I, J, and K are: ');
    WRITELN (I, J, K);
    WRITELN('The value of X is: ',X);
    WRITELN('The value of Y is: ',Y);
    WRITELN('The value of Z is: ',Z);
END.
```

4. Run the program.

```
Command: E(dit, R(un, F(ile, C(omp, X(ecute, U(ser restart [ED 1R0.0]
Running...
The values of I, J, and K are: 312210904212
The value of X is: 3.10450E3
The value of Y is: 1.09850E3
The value of Z is: 4.20300E3
```

The computer has used one space per digit and run all three numbers together on the screen. This is not a readable display. One way to improve the readability would be to output commas and spaces between the numbers.

5. Enter the Editor and recall your program.

6. Modify the WRITELN statement for I, J and K to read:

   WRITELN (I,', ', J,', ', K);

7. Run the program.

```
Command: E(dit, R(un, F(ile, C(omp, X(ecute, U(ser restart [ED 1R0.0]
Running...
The values of I, J, and K are: 3123, 1090, 4212
The value of X is: 3.10450E3
The value of Y is: 1.09850E3
The value of Z is: 4.20300E3
```

This technique provides a more readable presentation, especially when the numbers are to be presented in a row or sentence.

Adjust Column Width It is often necessary to produce columns of numbers on the page. The method of placing spaces between numbers in the previous example will line up columns only if the numbers all have the same number of digits. This is not a valid assumption in most cases. You often must print lists of numbers of varying lengths.

The WRITE and WRITELN statements allow you to specify a column length for each variable to be printed.

1. Enter the Editor and recall the program MATH.

2. Change the WRITE statement to a WRITELN statement.

3. Replace the statement: **WRITELN (I,', ', J,', ', K);** with the statements:

   WRITELN (I:6);
   WRITELN (J:6);
   WRITELN (K:6);

   and accept your insertion.

```
>Edit: A(djust C(opy D(el F(ind I(nsert J(ump K(ol M(argin P(age ? [ED 1R0.0]
PROGRAM MATH;

VAR X, Y, Z : REAL;
    I, J, K : INTEGER;

BEGIN
    I:=3925 + 87 - 2015 DIV 90 * 45 + 100;
    J:=((((3925 + 87) - 2015) DIV 90) * 45) + 100;
    K:=I + J;
    X:=3925.0 + 87.0 - 2015.0 / 90.0 * 45.0 + 100.0;
    Y:=(((((3925.0 + 87.0) - 2015.0) / 90.0) * 45.0) + 100.0);
    Z:=X + Y;
    WRITELN ('The values of I, J, and K are: ');
    WRITELN (I:6);
    WRITELN (J:6);
    WRITELN (K:6);
    WRITELN('The value of X is: ',X);
    WRITELN('The value of Y is: ',Y);
    WRITELN('The value of Z is: ',Z);
END.
```

4. Run the program.

```
Command: E(dit, R(un, F(ile, C(omp, X(ecute, U(ser restart [ED 1R0.0]
Running...
The values of I, J, and K are:
  3122
  1090
  4212
The value of X is: 3.10450E3
The value of Y is: 1.09850E3
The value of Z is: 4.20300E3
```

The three integer values are not printed in the first available space on the screen. There are two blank spaces, then four digits. This is because you specified a field length of 6. The values are right justified in the field. Unused columns are filled by spaces.

Formatting three values all the same length is easy. You could have ignored the column width in this case and had satisfactory results. Take a look at what happens when the numbers are different lengths.

5. Enter the Editor and recall your program to the display.

6. Replace the assignment statements for I, J, and K with:

   I:=18462;
   J:=12;
   K:=396;

```
>Edit: A(djust C(opy D(el F(ind I(nsert J(ump K(ol M(argin P(age ? [ED 1R0.0]
PROGRAM MATH;

VAR X, Y, Z : REAL;
    I, J, K : INTEGER;

BEGIN
    I:=18462;
    J:=12;
    K:=396;
    X:=3925.0 + 87.0 - 2015.0 / 90.0 * 45.0 + 100.0;
    Y:=(((((3925.0 + 87.0) - 2015.0) / 90.0) * 45.0) + 100.0);
    Z:=X + Y;
    WRITELN ('The values of I, J, and K are: ');
    WRITELN (I:6);
    WRITELN (J:6);
    WRITELN (K:6);
    WRITELN('The value of X is: ',X);
    WRITELN('The value of Y is: ',Y);
    WRITELN('The value of Z is: ',Z);
END.
```

7. Run the program.

```
Command: E(dit, R(un, F(ile, C(omp, X(ecute, U(ser restart [ED 1R0.0]
Running...
The values of I, J, and K are:
 18462
    12
   396
The value of X is: 3.10450E3
The value of Y is: 1.09850E3
The value of Z is: 4.20300E3
```

The values have appeared neatly right-justified in a 6-position field.

Default Real Formatting Unless you instruct otherwise, REAL values are printed in exponential notation. While exponential, or scientific, notation is useful for many applications, decimal notation is more appropriate much of the time.

Adjusting Column Width of Real Numbers You can attach a column width specification to a REAL variable in exactly the same manner as you attached a column width to the INTEGER variables.

1. Enter the Editor and call up your program.

```
>Edit: A(djust C(opy D(el F(ind I(nsert J(ump K(ol M(argin P(age ? [ED 1R0.0]
PROGRAM MATH;

VAR X, Y, Z : REAL;
    I, J, K : INTEGER;

BEGIN
    I:=18462;
    J:=12;
    K:=396;
    X:=3925.0 + 87.0 - 2015.0 / 90.0 * 45.0 + 100.0;
    Y:=(((((3925.0 + 87.0) - 2015.0) / 90.0) * 45.0) + 100.0);
    Z:=X + Y;
    WRITELN ('The values of I, J, and K are: ');
    WRITELN (I:6);
    WRITELN (J:6);
    WRITELN (K:6);
    WRITELN('The value of X is: ',X);
    WRITELN('The value of Y is: ',Y);
    WRITELN('The value of Z is: ',Z);
END.
```

To illustrate the effect of placing a column length specifier on the variables, print each variable twice. Print it once with the default format (exponential notation), and once with a column width designator. That way, you can readily compare the effect of adding the column length designator to the REAL variables.

2. Change the WRITELN statements for X, Y, and Z to read:

   WRITELN('The value of X is: ',X,**X:8**);
   WRITELN('The value of Y is: ',Y,**Y:8**);
   WRITELN('The value of Z is: ',Z,**Z:8**);

```
>Edit: A(djust C(opy D(el F(ind I(nsert J(ump K(ol M(argin P(age ? [ED 1R0.0]
PROGRAM MATH;

VAR X, Y, Z : REAL;
    I, J, K : INTEGER;

BEGIN
    I:=18462;
    J:=12;
    K:=396;
    X:=3925.0 + 87.0 - 2015.0 / 90.0 * 45.0 + 100.0;
    Y:=(((((3925.0 + 87.0) - 2015.0) / 90.0) * 45.0) + 100.0);
    Z:=X + Y;
    WRITELN ('The values of I, J, and K are: ');
    WRITELN (I:6);
    WRITELN (J:6);
    WRITELN (K:6);
    WRITELN('The value of X is: ',X,X:8);
    WRITELN('The value of Y is: ',Y,Y:8);
    WRITELN('The value of Z is: ',Z,Z:8);
END.
```

3. Run the program.

```
Command: E(dit, R(un, F(ile, C(omp, X(ecute, U(ser restart [ED 1R0.0]
Running...
The values of I, J, and K are:
 18462
    12
   396
The value of X is: 3.10450E3    3105
The value of Y is: 1.09850E3    1098
The value of Z is: 4.20300E3    4203
```

The REAL numbers are formatted to your column width specification of eight columns. Following the exponential form of the number are four blank spaces and then four digits. No numbers are printed to the right of the decimal place.

All REAL values are rounded before printing. If the digit past the last digit printed is greater than 5, the number is rounded up. If the digit is less than 5, five, the number is rounded down. The number 3105 in the output above has been rounded up. The number 1098 was rounded down. This does not appear to be correct or consistent because in the exponential form, both numbers have "50" as the last two digits. What you must remember, however, is that the exponential notation is also rounded before being printed. The numbers printed are actually correct and consistent.

Decimal Places An additional specification can be added to provide for decimal places. Revise the program to print the REAL values with decimal digits. To make the comparison easier, add an additional field instead of modifying an existing one.

1. Enter the Editor.

2. Change the WRITELN statements for X, Y, and Z to read:

   WRITELN('The value of X is: ',X,X:8,**X:8:2**);
   WRITELN('The value of Y is: ',Y,Y:8,**Y:8:2**);
   WRITELN('The value of Z is: ',Z,Z:8,**Z:8:2**);

3. Run the program.

```
Command: E(dit, R(un, F(ile, C(omp, X(ecute, U(ser restart [ED 1R0.0]
Running...
The values of I, J, and K are:
 18462
    12
   396
The value of X is: 3.10450E3    3105 3104.50
The value of Y is: 1.09850E3    1098 1098.50
The value of Z is: 4.20300E3    4203 4203.00
```

The third column of REAL values occupies a total field width of eight spaces. The first space is reserved for the sign. In the example, all the numbers are positive, therefore the sign position is blank. When planning REAL output, consider that the total field width consists of one sign space, digits to the left of the decimal place, the decimal point, and digits to the right of the decimal point.

If you do not specify a large enough field width, the program will ignore your column width specification and print the number in exponential notation. This will prevent proper alignment of decimal numbers.

Default String Formatting STRING variables change length as the program is run. If you do not specify a length in the WRITE or WRITELN statement, the STRING value will occupy as many spaces as necessary on the screen.

1. Enter the Filer, use the N(ew command to clear the workfile, and return to the main command line.
2. Enter the Editor and begin a new program. Name it STROUT for "string output."
3. Declare LINE as a variable of type STRING.

```
>Insert: Text {<bs> a char, <del> a line} [<ext> accepts, <esc> escapes]
PROGRAM STROUT;

VAR LINE : STRING;
```

4. Assign the string "An ill wind blows no good." to LINE.
5. Use the WRITELN statements to display LINE with:

- No field width specifier
- A field width of 50
- A field width of 17.

```
>Insert: Text {<bs> a char, <del> a line} [<ext> accepts, <esc> escapes]
PROGRAM STROUT;

VAR LINE : STRING;

BEGIN
    LINE:='An ill wind blows no good.';
    WRITELN(LINE);
    WRITELN(LINE:50);
    WRITELN(LINE:17);
END.
```

6. Run the program.

```
Command: E(dit, R(un, F(ile, C(omp, X(ecute, U(ser restart [ED 1R0.0]
Running...
An ill wind blows no good.
                                An ill wind blows no good.

An ill wind blows
```

The first WRITELN places the string in the first 26 spaces on the screen. The second WRITELN statement right-justifies the string in a 50-space field and pads the leftmost positions with blanks. The third WRITELN displays the leftmost 17 characters of the string in the first 17 spaces on the screen.

WHAT YOU HAVE LEARNED

- Create WRITE parameter list
- Default INTEGER formatting
- Default REAL formatting
- Adjust column width
- Adjust decimal position

REVIEW

1. Any output entry not enclosed in quotation marks is considered by the computer to be what kind of information?

2. How many spaces does default INTEGER formatting use?

3. How can you make a default INTEGER formatting become more readable?

4. How can you right-justify a column of INTEGER values?

5. What does default REAL formatting produce?

6. When formatting REAL variables what is the purpose of having two fields?

7. Is it necessary to specify a variable length for a STRING variable?

8. What happens if a variable field longer then the STRING variable is specified in a WRITELN statement?

9. What happens if the field width for a STRING is too short?

PART 12
INPUT STATEMENTS

WHAT YOU WILL LEARN

- Keyboard input of single numbers with READLN
- Type matching
- Keyboard input of CHAR variables with READLN
- Keyboard input of CHAR variables with READ
- Keyboard input of STRING variables

Module 22
SINGLE NUMBER KEYBOARD INPUT

KEY TOPICS

- Keyboard input of single numbers with READLN
- Type matching

PRACTICE SESSION

Specifying numerical input from the keyboard requires a new statement that tells the computer to expect this information.

PREPARATION Enter the Filer, set the system date, and clear the workfile. Return to the command line.

LEARNING ACTIVITY All the programming activities so far have required you to place input values directly into the Pascal source program. For programs to be flexible and useable by someone other than the programmer who wrote them, they must be capable of accepting input from the keyboard and other devices.

The READLN Statement The primary input mechanism for accepting input from a program user is the keyboard. The READLN statement is the most useful Pascal statement for accepting user input from the keyboard.

As an example, create a program to compute the diameter, circumference, and area of a circle when the user provides the radius.

1. Enter the Editor. Name your program CIRCLES.

2. Declare the constant PI equal to 3.14159. Declare the variables RADIUS, DIAMETER, CIRCUMFERENCE, and AREA as REAL.

```
>Insert: Text {<bs> a char, <del> a line} [<ext> accepts, <esc> escapes]
PROGRAM CIRCLES;

CONST PI=3.14159;

VAR RADIUS, DIAMETER, CIRCUMFERENCE, AREA:REAL;
```

3. Add assignment statements to compute the diameter, circumference, and area.

DIAMETER:= RADIUS * 2.0;
CIRCUMFERENCE:= DIAMETER * PI;
AREA:= PI * RADIUS * RADIUS;

4. Add WRITELN statements to display RADIUS, DIAMETER, CIRCUMFERENCE, and AREA. Provide meaningful labels for your variables, and display them in decimal format.

```
>Insert: Text {<bs> a char, <del> a line} [<ext> accepts, <esc> escapes]
PROGRAM CIRCLES;

CONST PI=3.14159;

VAR RADIUS, DIAMETER, CIRCUMFERENCE, AREA:REAL;

BEGIN
    DIAMETER:= RADIUS * 2.0;
    CIRCUMFERENCE:= DIAMETER * PI;
    AREA:= PI * RADIUS * RADIUS;
    WRITELN('The radius of the circle is:',RADIUS:10:5);
    WRITELN('The diameter of the circle is:',DIAMETER:10:5);
    WRITELN('The circumference of the circle is:',CIRCUMFERENCE:10:5);
    WRITELN('The area of the circle is:',AREA:10:5);
END.
```

The only value which remains undefined is the RADIUS. There are two steps involved in getting an input value from the keyboard. The first step is to display a message on the screen which informs the user that the program requires a value to be entered at the keyboard. The second step is to read the keyboard.

5. Add the statements:

   WRITE('Type the measure of the radius, then press Enter: ');
   READLN(RADIUS);

between the BEGIN statement and the computation of DIAMETER.

```
>Insert: Text {<bs> a char, <del> a line} [<ext> accepts, <esc> escapes]
PROGRAM CIRCLES;

CONST PI=3.14159;

VAR RADIUS, DIAMETER, CIRCUMFERENCE, AREA:REAL;

BEGIN
    WRITE('Type the measure of the radius, then press Enter: ');
    READLN(RADIUS);
    DIAMETER:= RADIUS * 2.0;
    CIRCUMFERENCE:= DIAMETER * PI;
    AREA:= PI * RADIUS * RADIUS;
    WRITELN('The radius of the circle is:',RADIUS:10:5);
    WRITELN('The diameter of the circle is:',DIAMETER:10:5);
    WRITELN('The circumference of the circle is:',CIRCUMFERENCE:10:5);
    WRITELN('The area of the circle is:',AREA:10:5);
END.
```

The WRITE statement informs the user of what is required. The READLN accepts the input.

6. Run the program.

```
Running...
Type the measure of the radius, then press Enter:_
```

The computer stops when it comes to the READLN statement and waits for you to enter a value.

7. Type **23** and press **Enter**.

```
Command: E(dit, R(un, F(ile, C(omp, X(ecute, U(ser restart [ED 1R0.0]
Running
Type the measure of the radius, then press Enter:23
The value of the radius is:   23.0000
The value of the diameter is:  46.0000
The value of the circumference is:  144.513
The value of the area is: 1661.90
```

To use the program again with a new value, run it again. Notice that the computer does not have to recompile your program.

8. Type **R** for Run.

```
Running...
Type the measure of the radius, then press Enter:_
```

9. Type **0.3** and press **Enter**.

```
Command: E(dit, R(un, F(ile, C(omp, X(ecute, U(ser restart [ED 1R0.0]
Running
Type the measure of the radius, then press Enter:0.3
The value of the radius is:    0.30000
The value of the diameter is:  0.60000
The value of the circumference is:  1.88495
The value of the area is:   0.28274
```

Type Matching The computer is not picky just about variable types when making assignments or performing computations. It also enforces the rules when getting input from the keyboard.

1. Type **R** for Run.

```
Running...
Type the measure of the radius, then press Enter:_
```

2. Type **K**.

"K" is not a valid number. The computer objects immediately.

```
Running...
Type the measure of the radius, then press Enter:_


IO error: bad input format--Seg CIRCLES P# 1 O# 24 <space> continues_
```

3. Press **Spacebar** to restart the system.

```
Command: E(dit, R(un, F(ile, C(omp, X(ecute, U(ser restart [ED 1R0.0]
System re-initialized
```

The computer is not picky just about REAL input. It objects just as forcefully to illegal characters in INTEGER input, although it is tolerant of decimal points in INTEGER input. Decimals in INTEGER input do not abort the program, they are simply ignored. In later modules, you will learn a variety of techniques to recover gracefully from bad keyboard input.

WHAT YOU HAVE LEARNED

- Keyboard input of single numbers with READLN
- Type matching

REVIEW

1. What is the purpose of the READLN statement?

2. What does the computer do when it comes to a READLN statement?

3. How does the computer react when it receives a variable value that is inconsistent with the variable type?

Module 23
INPUT A CHARACTER

KEY TOPICS

- Keyboard input of CHAR variables with READLN
- Keyboard input of CHAR variables with READ
- Keyboard input of STRING variables

PRACTICE SESSION

Input of characters is done in the same way as input of numbers. Characters as input permit greater flexibility in program output.

PREPARATION Display the main command line on your computer console.

LEARNING ACTIVITY Numbers are not the only elements that can be entered into a program from the keyboard. Characters can also be entered.

Keyboard Input of CHAR Variables with READLN A variable of type CHAR is useful for providing short answers. In your use of the p-System, you have used single character input to move from the command line to other parts of the p-System and back again.

1. Enter the Editor and create a new program called SHORT.
2. Declare the variable "C" to be of type CHAR.
3. Input a value for the variable "C" with the READLN statement.
4. Display the value of "C" with the WRITELN statement.

```
>Edit: A(djust C(opy D(el F(ind I(nsert J(ump K(ol M(argin P(age ? [ED 1R0.0]
PROGRAM SHORT;

VAR C:CHAR;

BEGIN
    WRITE('Type a character, then press ENTER ');
    READLN(C);
    WRITELN('The character you typed was ',C);
END.
```

5. Run the program.

```
Running...
Type a character, then press ENTER _
```

6. Type **K** and press **Enter**.

```
Command: E(dit, R(un, F(ile, C(omp, X(ecute, U(ser restart [ED 1R0.0]
Running...
Type a character, then press Enter K
The character you typed was K
```

The computer responds exactly as expected, echoing your letter onto the screen.

7. Run the program again.

```
Running...
Type a character, then press ENTER _
```

8. Type the number **8** and press **Enter**.

```
Command: E(dit, R(un, F(ile, C(omp, X(ecute, U(ser restart [ED 1R0.0]
Running...
Type a character, then press Enter 8
The character you typed was 8
```

Remember that numbers are also characters.

9. Run the program again. Enter the plus sign, +.

```
Command: E(dit, R(un, F(ile, C(omp, X(ecute, U(ser restart [ED 1R0.0]
Running...
Type a character, then press Enter +
The character you typed was +
```

Letters, numbers, and special symbols are all valid input to a CHAR variable.

Keyboard Input of CHAR Variables with READ The input statement in program SHORT does not behave exactly like the input statement that makes the p-System command line work. In your program, you must press **Enter** after typing your answer. Pascal provides the READ statement to input from the keyboard and does not require you to press **Enter**.

1. Enter the Editor, recalling program SHORT.

2. Change the READLN statement to a READ statement.

3. Change the first WRITE statement to display only "Type a character."

```
>Edit: A(djust C(opy D(el F(ind I(nsert J(ump K(ol M(argin P(age ? [ED 1R0.0]
PROGRAM SHORT;

VAR C:CHAR;

BEGIN
    WRITE('Type a character ');
    READ(C);
    WRITE('The character you typed was ',C);
END.
```

4. Run the program.

```
Running...
Type a character _
```

5. Type **P**.

```
Command: E(dit, R(un, F(ile, C(omp, X(ecute, U(ser restart [ED 1R0.0]
Running...
Type a character PThe character you typed was P
```

The computer did not require you to press **Enter** before accepting your input. As a result, the cursor was not repositioned at the start of the next line. The second line of output is displayed immediately following the first line.

It is not necessary to use a READLN statement to move the cursor to the next line. A WRITELN statement could be added to accomplish the same thing.

6. Add a WRITELN statement after the READ statement.

```
>Edit: A(djust C(opy D(el F(ind I(nsert J(ump K(ol M(argin P(age ? [ED 1R0.0]
PROGRAM SHORT;

VAR C:CHAR;

BEGIN
    WRITE('Type a character ');
    READ(C);
    WRITELN;
    WRITE('The character you typed was ',C);
END.
```

7. Run the program, responding with the character **q**.

```
Command:  E(dit,  R(un,  F(ile,  C(omp,  X(ecute,  U(ser restart [ED 1R0.0]
Running...
Type a character q
The character you typed was q
```

The program output is now the same as it was before. In using the READ statement, you have saved the program user an additional keystroke.

Using the READ statement to input values from the keyboard is primarily useful with variables of type CHAR. It can be used with INTEGER and REAL input, but it is difficult to protect the program from accidental type mismatch errors. The READ statement can not be used to input STRING variables from the keyboard.

Keyboard Input of String Variables STRING values can be entered from the keyboard through the use of the READLN statement.

1. Enter the Filer and clear the workfile.

2. Enter the Editor and create program INSTRING.

3. Declare SENTENCE as a variable of type STRING.

4. Input SENTENCE from the keyboard using the READLN statement and display it on the screen using WRITE.

```
>Edit: A(djust C(opy D(el F(ind I(nsert J(ump K(ol M(argin P(age ? [ED 1R0.0]
PROGRAM INSTRING;

VAR SENTENCE:STRING;

BEGIN
    WRITELN('Type a sentence, then press Enter. ');
    READLN(SENTENCE);
    WRITELN('Your sentence is:');
    WRITE(SENTENCE);
END.
```

5. Run the program.

```
Running...
Type a sentence, then press Enter.

_
```

6. Type **That's one small step for a man, one giant leap for mankind.** and press **Enter**.

```
Command: E(dit, R(un, F(ile, C(omp, X(ecute, U(ser restart [ED 1R0.0]
Running...
Type a sentence, then press Enter.
That's one small step for a man, one giant leap for mankind.
Your sentence is:
That's one small step for a man, one giant leap for mankind.
```

WHAT YOU HAVE LEARNED

- Keyboard input of CHAR variables with READLN
- Keyboard input of CHAR variables with READ
- Keyboard input of STRING variables

REVIEW

1. Write a VAR statement which defines "X" as a character.

2. How is the READ statement different from the READLN statement?

3. What is the advantage of using a READ statement and then a WRITELN statement?

4. Why can't you use the READ statement to input STRING variables?

PART 13
BRANCHING STATEMENTS

WHAT YOU WILL LEARN

- Evaluate BOOLEAN variables
- BOOLEAN operators
- Use IF THEN statement
- Use IF THEN statement with BEGIN END group
- Use ELSE clause
- Use nested IF construct
- CASE statement with simple statements
- CASE statement with procedures
- CASE statement with BEGIN END groups

Module 24
BOOLEAN VARIABLES

KEY TOPICS

- Evaluate BOOLEAN variables
- BOOLEAN operators

PRACTICE SESSION

This module helps you to understand how to make comparisons in mathematical equations.

PREPARATION There is no special preparation for this module.

LEARNING ACTIVITY All the programs you have written so far have performed operations as a sequence of linear steps. There has been no facility to change the order of operations, or to specify different operations depending on different conditions or different user input.

Pascal provides several statements to alter the execution of a program while it is running. Many of these techniques are based on the use of BOOLEAN variables. A BOOLEAN variable has two possible values, TRUE and FALSE.

There are two ways to assign a value to a BOOLEAN variable. If DONE is declared as a BOOLEAN variable in your program, the statement "DONE:=TRUE;" assigns the value TRUE to DONE. The second way to assign a value is through the use of a BOOLEAN expression.

BOOLEAN Comparisons The comparisons available to form BOOLEAN expressions using INTEGER, REAL, CHAR, and STRING variables are:

=   equal to
<> not equal to
>   greater than
>= greater than or equal to
<   less than
<= less than or equal to

The operators available to form BOOLEAN expressions are:

NOT	negation
AND	conjunction
OR	union

BOOLEAN operators have an order of precedence. NOT operations are performed first, followed in order by AND, then OR. Parentheses may be used to alter the order of precedence.

If you define TEST as a BOOLEAN variable:

TEST:= 5<10;	{Assigns TRUE to TEST because 5<10 is a true statement}
TEST:= 3>17;	{Assigns FALSE to TEST because 17 is greater than three}
TEST:= 3>1 and 5>6;	{Assigns FALSE to TEST. Although 3>1 is true, both parts of an AND operation must be true to make the statement true. 5>6 is false; therefore, the entire statement is false.}
TEST:= 3>1 OR 5>6;	{Assigns TRUE to TEST. Only one of the expressions in an OR comparison must be true to make the entire statement true.}
TEST:= 5=5;	{Assigns the value TRUE to TEST, because 5 is equal to itself.}
TEST:= NUM=17	{If NUM=17 is a true statement, TRUE is assigned to TEST. If NUM is not equal to 17, then FALSE is assigned to TEST. This statement does *not* assign the number 17 to NUM. Do not confuse the assignment operator (:=) and the BOOLEAN equal sign (:=).}

WHAT YOU HAVE LEARNED

- Evaluate BOOLEAN variables
- BOOLEAN operators

REVIEW

1. What is the symbol for "not equal to"?

2. What is the symbol for "less than or equal to"?

3. What is the order of precedence for the BOOLEAN operators?

4. What are the two possible values of a BOOLEAN variable?

Module 25
IF THEN

KEY TOPICS

- Use IF THEN statement
- Use IF THEN statement with BEGIN END group
- Use ELSE clause
- Use nested IF construct

PRACTICE SESSION

Using statements that test for minimum and maximum limits of variables may seem complicated but it is very logical. Programs that incorporate statements to check if something is true or false before performing an operation are easy to understand and create.

PREPARATION Your computer console should show the main command line.

LEARNING ACTIVITY The IF statement allows the programmer to control the performance of program statements depending on the value of a BOOLEAN variable or expression.

The Hydalec Company, a seaweed sandwich company, pays its seaweed harvesters in clams. The basic pay rate is six clams an hour, based on a 40-hour workweek. For any hours over 40, the harvesters are paid nine clams an hour. The company only pays for whole hours worked. That way their labor doesn't cost as much. The company has decided to computerize its payroll and requires a program to compute wages.

1. Enter the Editor and create a program named PAYROLL.

2. Declare the variables HOURS and CLAMS as INTEGER.

3. Use a READLN statement to accept the hours worked from the keyboard.

```
>Insert: Text {<bs> a char, <del> a line} [<ext> accepts, <esc> escapes]
PROGRAM PAYROLL;

VAR HOURS, CLAMS: INTEGER;

BEGIN
    WRITE('How many hours were worked? ');
    READLN(HOURS);
```

There are two categories of harvesters, those working more than 40-hours per week and those working 40 or fewer hours per week. You need a separate formula to figure the number of clams to pay each class of workers. There are several ways to do this, but one way would be to use two IF THEN statements.

4. Add the IF statements below to your program:
   IF HOURS <= 40 THEN CLAMS:= HOURS * 6;
   IF HOURS > 40 THEN CLAMS:= 40 * 6 + (HOURS–40) * 9;

5. Add a WRITE statement to display the number of clams.

```
>Insert: Text {<bs> a char, <del> a line} [<ext> accepts, <esc> escapes]
PROGRAM PAYROLL;

VAR HOURS, CLAMS: INTEGER;

BEGIN
    WRITE('How many hours were worked? ');
    READLN(HOURS);
    IF HOURS <= 40 THEN CLAMS:= HOURS * 6;
    IF HOURS > 40 THEN CLAMS:= 40 * 6 + (HOURS-40) * 9;
    WRITE('Pay this harvester ',CLAMS,' clams.');
END.
```

6. Run the program.

```
Running...
How many hours were worked? _
```

7. Type **32** and press **Enter**.

```
Command: E(dit, R(un, F(ile, C(omp, X(ecute, U(ser restart [ED 1R0.0]
Running...
How many hours were worked? 32
Pay this harvester 192 clams.
```

The test of the first IF statement, HOURS <= 40, evaluates to TRUE, and therefore the assignment statement CLAMS:= HOURS * 6 is executed. The test of the second IF statement, HOURS > 40, evaluates to FALSE; therefore its assignment statement is not executed, and the value of CLAMS remains 192.

8. Run the program. Enter **47** hours.

```
Command: E(dit, R(un, F(ile, C(omp, X(ecute, U(ser restart [ED 1R0.0]
Running...
How many hours were worked? 47
Pay this harvester 303 clams.
```

The test of the first IF statement, HOURS <= 40, evaluates to FALSE, and its assignment statement is not performed. The test of the second IF, HOURS > 40, evaluates to TRUE, therefore its assignment statement is executed, and the 303 is assigned to CLAMS.

9. Run the program several more times with different numbers of hours.

ELSE Many times you want to test conditions where the alternatives are mutually exclusive. The IF THEN statement has an ELSE option to make it easier to express this concept.

1. Enter the Editor and recall program PAYROLL.

```
>Edit: A(djust C(opy D(el F(ind I(nsert J(ump K(ol M(argin P(age ? [ED 1R0.0]
PROGRAM PAYROLL;

VAR HOURS, CLAMS: INTEGER;

BEGIN
    WRITE('How many hours were worked? ');
    READLN(HOURS);
    IF HOURS <=40 THEN CLAMS:= HOURS * 6;
    IF HOURS > 40 THEN CLAMS:= 40 * 6 + (HOURS-40) * 9;
    WRITE('Pay this harvester ',CLAMS,' clams.');
END.
```

The two IF statements test for mutually exclusive conditions. If the number of hours is less than 40, there is no reason to test to see if it is greater than or equal to 40. While the procedure in this program works, the code is cumbersome, unclear, and can lead to mistakes. The ELSE clause on the IF statement provides a way to perform one test, then take one action if the test is true, another if the test is false.

2. Delete the second IF statement.

3. Modify the first IF statement to read:

```
IF HOURS <= 40 THEN
     CLAMS := HOURS * 6
ELSE
       CLAMS := 40 * 6 + (HOURS-40) * 9;
```

Notice that there is no longer a semicolon after "CLAMS := HOURS * 6." In Pascal, semicolons appear at the ends of statements. This entire expression is one statement. A complex statement to be sure, but a single statement. The semicolon appears at the end of the statement, following the second assignment statement.

```
>Insert: Text {<bs> a char, <del> a line} [<ext> accepts, <esc> escapes]
PROGRAM PAYROLL;

VAR HOURS, CLAMS: INTEGER;

BEGIN
    WRITE('How many hours were worked? ');
    READLN(HOURS);
    IF HOURS <= 40 THEN
        CLAMS := HOURS * 6
    ELSE
        CLAMS := 40 * 6 + (HOURS-40) * 9;
    WRITE('Pay this harvester ',CLAMS,' clams.');
END.
```

This revision makes it easier to understand that only one of the assignment statements will be performed.

4. Run the program several times. Verify that the change in the program has not affected the output.

Nested IF Statements The example you are working on performs assignment statements as the result of an IF test. In fact, any valid Pascal statement may be performed as the result of an IF test, including another IF statement.

1. Run the program.

```
Running...
How many hours were worked? _
```

2. Type **−57** and press **Enter**.

```
Command: E(dit, R(un, F(ile, C(omp, X(ecute, U(ser restart [ED 1R0.0]
Running...
How many hours were worked? -57
Pay this harvester -342 clams.
```

The result of this program run is garbage. The computer performed exactly as instructed by the program. In practice, however, it is not possible to work a negative number of hours. The computer has accepted this number, performed calculations based on it, and presents you with the results.

A well-designed program should not do this. When given an input value that is not reasonable, the computer should inform the user the input value is bad, and not perform the calculations. In this case, an IF statement can be used to check the data for reasonableness. It is not possible for a worker to work fewer than 0 hours in a week. Seven days of 24 hours per day is 168 hours. It is unlikely that any worker would work that many, but it is certainly impossible for a worker to work more than 168 hours in a single week.

3. Modify the program as shown:

```
PROGRAM PAYROLL;

VAR HOURS, CLAMS: INTEGER;

BEGIN
    WRITE('How many hours were worked? ');
    READLN(HOURS);
    IF (HOURS < 0) OR (HOURS > 168) THEN
        WRITELN('The number of hours is invalid.')
    ELSE
        IF HOURS <= 40 THEN
            CLAMS := HOURS * 6
        ELSE
            CLAMS := 40 * 6 + (HOURS-40) * 9;
    WRITE('Pay this harvester ',CLAMS,' clams.');
END.
```

4. Run the program. Specify **−18** hours.

```
Command: E(dit, R(un, F(ile, C(omp, X(ecute, U(ser restart [ED 1R0.0]
Running...
How many hours were worked? -18
The number of hours is invalid.
Pay this harvester 0 clams.
```

Close, but not quite. The new program logic has correctly identified the invalid input and has bypassed the calculations. As a result, no value is assigned to the variable CLAMS. However, the statement "WRITE ('Pay this harvester ',CLAMS,' clams.');" is still executed. This statement should be executed only when the input is valid. The value of CLAMS is unpredictable and depends on the random contents of the computer's memory. This is certainly a condition to avoid.

BEGIN END Groups There are several methods which could be used to prevent the display of output based on invalid input. A poor method would be to make the WRITE statement the object of another "IF (HOURS < 0) OR (HOURS > 168)" statement. A better way is to incorporate the WRITE statement in the existing program logic. This can be accomplished by bundling a group of statements together in a BEGIN END group.

1. Enter the Editor, recalling your program.

2. Place the word BEGIN after the first ELSE statement.

3. Place the word END after the last WRITE statement.

```
PROGRAM PAYROLL;

VAR HOURS, CLAMS: INTEGER;

BEGIN
    WRITE('How many hours were worked? ');
    READLN(HOURS);
    IF (HOURS < 0) OR (HOURS > 168) THEN
        WRITELN('The number of hours is invalid.')
    ELSE
    BEGIN
        IF HOURS <= 40 THEN
            CLAMS := HOURS * 6
        ELSE
            CLAMS := 40 * 6 + (HOURS-40) * 9;
        WRITE('Pay this harvester ',CLAMS,' clams.');
    END
 END.
```

4. Run the program. Specify **-18** hours.

```
Command:  E(dit,  R(un, F(ile, C(omp, X(ecute, U(ser restart [ED 1R0.0]
Running...
How many hours were worked? -18
The number of hours is invalid.
```

The offending statement no longer appears in the output.

5. Run the program. Specify **51** hours.

```
Command: E(dit, R(un, F(ile, C(omp, X(ecute, U(ser restart [ED 1R0.0]
Running...
How many hours were worked? 51
Pay this harvester 339 clams.
```

The payment statement does appear when the input is reasonable.

You need this program in a later module.

6. Use the Filer T(ransfer command to transfer SYSTEM.WRK.TEXT to PAYROLL.TEXT.

WHAT YOU HAVE LEARNED

- Use IF THEN statement
- Use IF THEN statement with BEGIN END group
- Use ELSE clause
- Use nested IF construct

REVIEW

1. IF THEN statements test what kinds of expressions?

2. When is an ELSE statement performed?

3. Why is an ELSE statement better than two IF THEN statements?

4. How many nested IF THEN statements could you have in a program?

5. What is the purpose of BEGIN END groups?

Module 26
CASE STATEMENT

KEY TOPICS

- CASE statement with simple statements
- CASE statement with procedures
- CASE statement with BEGIN END groups

PRACTICE SESSION

In Module 25 you learned how to write IF THEN statements and combinations of IF THEN statements to make program decisions. This module introduces the CASE statement, a more powerful statement which can be used for more complex branches.

PREPARATION Set the system date. Access the Editor in preparation for writing a new program.

LEARNING ACTIVITY The IF statement is ideally suited for selecting one of two possible actions. In the PAYROLL program, all harvesters were classified into two groups, regular and overtime. Frequently, programs must handle decisions involving more than two classifications. An educational management program might perform different actions based on the classifications of freshman, sophomore, junior, senior, and special. A military program might want to distinguish general, colonel, major, captain, lieutenant and private.

The menus of the p-System provide an excellent example. When at the command line you have five options: Edit, Run, Filer, Compiler, and User Restart. If each of these were procedures, and the input from the user was done with a READ (CHOICE) where CHOICE was a CHAR variable, then the following program code segment could be used to make the decision about which procedure to execute:

```
READ (CHOICE);

IF CHOICE = /E" THEN
    EDITOR
ELSE
    IF CHOICE='R' THEN
        RUN
    ELSE
         IF CHOICE='F' THEN
             FILER
         ELSE
             IF CHOICE='C' THEN
                 COMPILER
             ELSE
                 IF CHOICE='U' THEN
                     RESTART;
```

Even with careful indention to improve readability, the structure above is difficult to follow. It would be easy to make errors in program coding. Using this technique for a longer menu, such as the Filer menu, would greatly compound the potential for confusion and error.

CASE Statement with Procedures Pascal provides the CASE statement to control multiple option decisions. Expressing this same program segment with a CASE structure would look like:

```
READ (CHOICE);

CASE CHOICE OF
     'R' : RUN;
     'F' : FILER;
     'C' : COMPILE;
     'U' : RESTART
END;
```

The CASE statement is much easier to code and infinitely more readable than the nested IF construction. The action of the statement is obvious at a glance; you do not have to study your way through multiple levels of IF statements to understand what it does.

Create a program to select one of five messages to place on the screen, based on user input.

1. Create program MESSAGE.

2. Define CHOICE as a CHAR variable.

3. Use a CASE statement to print one of five messages as shown.

```
>Insert: Text {<bs> a char, <del> a line} [<ext> accepts, <esc> escapes]
PROGRAM MESSAGE;

VAR CHOICE: CHAR;

BEGIN
     WRITE ('Press the letter of your choice, (A-E): ');
     READ(CHOICE);
     WRITELN;
     CASE CHOICE OF
       'A','a'  : WRITELN('A stitch in time saves nine.');
       'B','b'  : WRITELN('Don''t cry over spilt milk.');
       'C','c'  : WRITELN('Blood is thicker than water.');
       'D','d'  : WRITELN('The squeaky wheel gets the grease.');
       'E','e'  : WRITELN('A watched pot never boils.')
      END;
END.
```

4. Run the program.

5. Type **C**.

```
Command: E(dit, R(un, F(ile, C(omp, X(ecute, U(ser restart [ED 1R0.0]
Running...
Press the letter of your choice, (A-E): C
Blood is thicker than water.
```

6. Run the program. Type **b**.

```
Command: E(dit, R(un, F(ile, C(omp, X(ecute, U(ser restart [ED 1R0.0]
Running...
Press the letter of your choice, (A-E): b
Don't cry over spilt milk.
```

Notice the technique used to place the apostrophe in the word "Don't."

7. Run the program. Type **K**.

```
Command: E(dit, R(un, F(ile, C(omp, X(ecute, U(ser restart [ED 1R0.0]
Running...
Press the letter of your choice, (A-E): K
```

The program does not print a message. If a match is not found for one of the conditions specified in the CASE statement it does not produce an error. None of the options are performed, and control passes to the statement immediately following the CASE statement. In this program, it was the end of the program.

WHAT YOU HAVE LEARNED

- CASE statement with simple statements
- CASE statement with procedures
- CASE statement with BEGIN END groups

REVIEW

1. What is the advantage of a CASE statement over a nested IF statement?

2. When is it preferrable to use an IF statement instead of a CASE statement?

3. What happens if no match is found as an option in a CASE statement?

4. How could you make sure that the variable in a CASE statement would always have a match?

5. Write a CASE statement to print your choice of six automobiles based on the input of a CHAR variable containing the first letter of the brand. Available automobiles are Mercedes, Rolls Royce, Jaguar, Ferrari, Porsche, and Lamborghini.

PART 14
FOR LOOPS

WHAT YOU WILL LEARN

- Simple FOR TO statement
- Compound FOR TO statement
- Variables as start and end points
- FOR DOWNTO statement

Module 27
FOR LOOPS

Key Topics

- Simple FOR TO statement
- Compound FOR TO statement
- Variables as start and end points
- FOR DOWNTO statement

PRACTICE SESSION

One of the great strengths of computers is their capability to repeat a function many times. Pascal provides three looping structures: the WHILE loop, the REPEAT loop, and the FOR loop. Each of these structures is designed to solve a particular type of repetitive problem. Many looping problems can be solved with any of these loops, but by taking advantage of the subtle differences between them, you can make your programs easier to write, easier to read, and less prone to contain errors.

When working with loops of any kind, there are three conditions to watch for:

a. The first time through the loop
b. The last time through the loop
c. All other times through the loop

Many times, beginning programmers fail to consider all of these cases.

PREPARATION Use the Filer to clear the workfile. Enter the Editor and prepare to write a new program.

LEARNING ACTIVITY Sometimes you know in advance how many times you need to perform a function. An accounting program to generate end-of-year reports might have a function needing to be performed 12 times - once for each month.

As an example, print "I like Ike!" on the screen 14 times.

Simple FOR Statement This problem could be solved with 14 WRITELN statements, but that would be cumbersome. What if the problem were to print "I like Ike!" 10,000 times?

The FOR loop provides a straightforward solution to this problem.

The FOR loop requires a counter variable to keep track of how many times the loop has executed. The counter variable must be an ordinal variable. The only types of ordinal variable you have learned about are INTEGER and CHAR. Ordinal variables have "order." It makes sense to talk about the "next" INTEGER or the "next" character. The next INTEGER after 6 is 7. The next CHAR after L is M. REAL variables are not ordinal. It does not make sense to talk about the "next" REAL number because between any two REAL numbers there is always another number.

This problem requires that an action be performed 14 times. This could be done by having the action performed once for each letter from "A" to "M," but using the numbers 1 to 14 is more easily understood.

1. Name your program EISENHOWER.

2. Declare COUNT to be a variable of type INTEGER.

3. Use a FOR statement for the body of your program:
   FOR COUNT:= 1 TO 14 DO WRITELN ('I like Ike!');

```
>Edit: A(djust C(opy D(el F(ind I(nsert J(ump K(ol M(argin P(age ? [ED 1R0.0]
PROGRAM EISENHOWER;

VAR COUNT : INTEGER;

BEGIN
    FOR COUNT:= 1 TO 14 DO WRITELN ('I like Ike!');
END.
```

The functions of the FOR statement are

a. Assign the number one to COUNT.

b. Perform the WRITELN statement.

c. Set COUNT equal to the next number.

d. Check to see if COUNT is greater than 14.

e. If COUNT is not equal to 14, go to step b; otherwise go to the next statement.

4. Run the program.

```
Command: E(dit, R(un, F(ile, C(omp, X(ecute, U(ser restart [ED 1R0.0]
Running...
I like Ike!
I like Ike!
I like Ike!
I like Ike!
I like Ike!
I like Ike!
I like Ike!
I like Ike!
I like Ike!
I like Ike!
I like Ike!
I like Ike!
I like Ike!
I like Ike!
```

The WRITELN statement was executed once for each value from 1 through 14.

5. Enter the Editor, recalling your program to the screen.

There are other ways of repeating this loop 14 times. The value of COUNT could have ranged from 1241 to 1254. The effect would be the same. Or, character variables could be used. To illustrate this technique, instead of printing "I like Ike!" for values of COUNT from 1 through 14, print them seven times by by letting COUNT vary from A to G.

6. Change the declaration of COUNT to CHAR.

7. Change the FOR statement to go from A to G instead of 1 to 14.

```
>Edit: A(djust C(opy D(el F(ind I(nsert J(ump K(ol M(argin P(age ? [ED 1R0.0]
PROGRAM EISENHOWER;

VAR COUNT : CHAR;

BEGIN
    FOR COUNT:= 'A' TO 'G' DO WRITELN ('I like Ike!);
END.
```

8. Run the program.

```
Command: E(dit, R(un, F(ile, C(omp, X(ecute, U(ser restart [ED 1R0.0]
Running...
I like Ike!
I like Ike!
I like Ike!
I like Ike!
I like Ike!
I like Ike!
I like Ike!
```

Compound FOR Statement Sometimes, instead of repeating just a single statement you want to repeat a series of statements. The object of a FOR statement can be a BEGIN END group instead of a single statement.

As an example, write a program to print a list of the first 16 powers of 2. Print them on the display.

One procedure to solve this problem is:

a. Let RESULT be the variable that the current power of 2 is stored in.

b. Assign 1 to RESULT. (This takes care of the 'first-time-through case'.)

c. Repeat the following steps 16 times:

   Multiply RESULT by 2 and place the product back in RESULT.

   Print RESULT on the screen. (The first time this step is executed, RESULT will equal 2. Therefore, the first number will be 2 to the first power.)

d. End of program.

Because the problem requires repeating an action a specific number of times, the FOR loop is an ideal solution.

1. Clear the workspace and create a new program called TWOS.

Repeating the action 16 times can be best expressed using an INTEGER counter. Since this counter corresponds to the current power of 2, use POWER as the counter variable.

2. Declare POWER as a variable of type INTEGER.

The powers of 2 get large rapidly. Therefore a REAL variable is appropriate for holding the result of the calculations. Remember that only about the first 6 digits of the result will be reliable because of the limited accuracy of REAL numbers.

3. Declare RESULT as REAL.

```
>Insert: Text {<bs> a char, <del> a line} [<ext> accepts, <esc> escapes]
PROGRAM TWOS;
VAR POWER : INTEGER;
    RESULT: REAL;
```

4. Initialize the value of RESULT to 1.

5. Use a FOR statement with a BEGIN END group to implement the loop:

```
FOR POWER:= 1 TO 16 DO
BEGIN
        RESULT:= RESULT * 2;
        WRITELN(POWER:2,RESULT:10)
END;
```

The completed program looks like:

```
>Insert: Text {<bs> a char, <del> a line} [<ext> accepts, <esc> escapes]
PROGRAM TWOS;
VAR POWER : INTEGER;
    RESULT: REAL;

BEGIN
    RESULT:=1;
    FOR POWER:= 1 TO 16 DO
    BEGIN
        RESULT:= RESULT * 2;
        WRITELN(POWER:2,RESULT:10)
    END;
END.
```

6. Run the program.

```
Command: E(dit, R(un, F(ile, C(omp, X(ecute, U(ser restart [ED 1R0.0]
Running...
 1        2
 2        4
 3        8
 4       16
 5       32
 6       64
 7      128
 8      256
 9      512
10     1024
11     2048
12     4096
13     8192
14    16384
15    32768
16    65536
```

You can see that you could not have used an INTEGER variable to keep track of RESULT because the final two values are greater than MAXINT.

Variable Start and End Points The starting and ending values of the counter variable do not have to be constants; they can also be variables.

As an example, create a program to print selected letters of the alphabet based on user input.

1. Clear the workspace and create a new program, ALPHA.

2. Declare INITIAL, FINAL, and COUNTER as CHAR variables.

3. Use READLN statements to accept the values. Place all the input statements in a procedure by themselves.

4. Display all characters between INITIAL and FINAL on one line, not separated by spaces.

```
>Edit: A(djust C(opy D(el F(ind I(nsert J(ump K(ol M(argin P(age ? [ED 1R0.0]
PROGRAM ALPHA;

VAR INITIAL, FINAL, COUNTER: CHAR;

PROCEDURE VALUES;
BEGIN
    WRITE('Enter the starting value: ');
    READLN(INITIAL);
    WRITE('Enter the ending value: ');
    READLN(FINAL);
END;

BEGIN
    VALUES;
    FOR COUNTER:=INITIAL TO FINAL DO WRITE(COUNTER);
END.
```

5. Run the program.

6. Use **A** as the starting value and **M** as the ending value.

```
Command: E(dit, R(un, F(ile, C(omp, X(ecute, U(ser restart [ED 1R0.0]
Running...
Enter the starting value: A
Enter the ending value: M
ABCDEFGHIJKLM
```

The capital letters “A” through “M” are printed.

7. Run the program. Use **a** as the starting value and **x** as the ending value.

```
Command: E(dit, R(un, F(ile, C(omp, X(ecute, U(ser restart [ED 1R0.0]
Running...
Enter the starting value: a
Enter the ending value: x
abcdefghijklmnopqrstuvwx
```

8. Run the program. Use **1** as the starting value and **9** as the ending value.

```
Command: E(dit, R(un, F(ile, C(omp, X(ecute, U(ser restart [ED 1R0.0]
Running...
Enter the starting value: 1
Enter the ending value: 9
123456789
```

Remember that numbers are characters also!

9. Run the program. Use **X** as the starting value and **B** as the ending value.

```
Command: E(dit, R(un, F(ile, C(omp, X(ecute, U(ser restart [ED 1R0.0]
Running...
Enter the starting value: X
Enter the ending value: B
```

The FOR loop is not executed if the starting value is already past the ending value.

Changing Direction Now, change the program so that the list is produced in descending order. This can be accomplished by changing the word TO to DOWNTO in the FOR statement.

1. Enter the Editor, recalling your program.

2. Replace TO with DOWNTO.

```
>Edit: A(djust C(opy D(el F(ind I(nsert J(ump K(ol M(argin P(age ? [ED 1R0.0]
PROGRAM ALPHA;

VAR INITIAL, FINAL, COUNTER: CHAR;

PROCEDURE VALUES;
BEGIN
    WRITE('Enter the starting value: ');
    READLN(INITIAL);
    WRITE('Enter the ending value: ');
    READLN(FINAL);
```

```
END;

BEGIN
    VALUES;
    FOR COUNTER:=INITIAL DOWNTO FINAL DO WRITE(COUNTER);
END.
```

3. Run the program. Use **X** as the starting value and **B** as the ending value.

```
Command: E(dit, R(un, F(ile, C(omp, X(ecute, U(ser restart [ED 1R0.0]
Running...
Enter the starting value: X
Enter the ending value: B
XWVUTSRQPONMLKJIHGFEDCB
```

Depending on your choice of the word TO or DOWNTO in writing the program, the counter variable will either be increased or decreased each time through the loop.

WHAT YOU HAVE LEARNED

- Simple FOR TO statement
- Compound FOR TO statement
- Variables as start and end points
- FOR DOWNTO statement

REVIEW

1. What is the value of a FOR statement?

2. What is an ordinal variable?

3. Why aren't REAL variables ordinal?

4. What will a compound FOR statement do that a simple FOR statement won't?

5. What is the purpose of the word DOWNTO in a FOR statement?

6. What happens if the starting value is greater than the ending value in a FOR TO statement?

PART 15
REPEAT AND WHILE LOOPS

WHAT YOU WILL LEARN

- REPEAT loops
- IORESULT
- WHILE DO loops
- Avoiding infinite loops

Module 28
REPEAT LOOPS

KEY TOPICS

- REPEAT loops
- IORESULT

PRACTICE SESSION
The REPEAT looping structure allows you to repeat an operation over and over UNTIL some condition is satisfied.

PREPARATION Clear the workfile and set the system date. Quit the Filer and return to the main command line.

LEARNING ACTIVITY Many times a loop must be performed at least once, but it is impossible to determine in advance just how many times are necessary.

IORESULT In the modules about input statements and type matching, you brought your system to a screeching halt by entering a letter when the system expected a number. A more graceful solution to the problem of improper input is to "capture" the error in the program and repeat the input routine until the user enters valid input.

The system provides a predeclared identifier, IORESULT, which is set each time an input or output operation is performed. When an operation is performed successfully, IORESULT is set to zero. When a problem occurs, IORESULT is set to a nonzero number. When reading an INTEGER or REAL number and a letter is pressed, IORESULT is set to error code 14, meaning "Bad format: error in reading real or integer." Other error codes have meanings appropriate to other devices, such as a disk drive, modem, or printer. The important value, however, is the value zero.

It is possible for you to intercept I/O (Input/Output) errors in the program instead of letting these errors abnormally end the program and return you to the operating system. An easy way to do this is with a REPEAT loop and the IORESULT identifier.

It is also necessary to tell the compiler that you wish to do your own error handling. This is done with the compiler I/O check option, {$I }. If you do not specify anything, the compiler will assume you want it to generate I/O checking code, {$I+}. When you wish to do your own checking, change the compiler switch to {$I–} before the I/O statement.

Create a program to input an INTEGER I, gracefully recover from input errors, and print the number on the screen.

1. Create program GRACEFUL.

2. Declare I as an INTEGER variable.

```
>Insert: Text {<bs> a char, <del> a line} [<ext> accepts, <esc> escapes]
PROGRAM GRACEFUL;

VAR I:INTEGER;
```

3. Turn off the compiler I/O check options.

4. Add a REPEAT loop to do the input and checking.

5. Turn I/O checking back on.

6. Add a WRITELN to verify the input.

```
>Insert: Text {<bs> a char, <del> a line} [<ext> accepts, <esc> escapes]
PROGRAM GRACEFUL;

VAR I,ERROR_CODE : INTEGER;

BEGIN
    {$I-}
    REPEAT
        WRITE('Enter an integer: ');
        READ(I);
        ERROR_CODE:=IORESULT;
        READLN;
    UNTIL ERROR_CODE=0;
    {$I+}
    WRITELN('The integer you input was: ',I);
END.
```

The statement sequence:

```
READ(I);
ERROR CODE:=IORESULT;
READLN;
```

must be used to properly set IORESULT. Immediately after executing the READ statement, IORESULT is assigned to ERRORCODE. The READLN statement accepts the carriage return character that is produced when you press **Enter**.

7. Run the program.

8. Type **5** and press **Enter**.

```
Command: E(dit, R(un, F(ile, C(omp, X(ecute, U(ser restart [ED 1R0.0]
Running...
Enter an integer: 5
The integer you input was: 5
```

The program works well with valid input. Now try giving the program some invalid input data.

9. Run the program. Type **K** and press **Enter**.

```
Running...
Enter an integer: K
Enter an integer: _
```

The program has failed to accept your invalid input. However, instead of abnormally terminating the program and returning to the command line, your program has intercepted the error and repeated the input request.

10. Type **hello** and press **Enter**.

```
Running...
Enter an integer: K
Enter an integer: hello
Enter an integer: _
```

The program will continuously repeat its request for an integer until you supply a value it can interpret properly.

11. Type **8.794** and press **Enter**.

```
Command: E(dit, R(un, F(ile, C(omp, X(ecute, U(ser restart [ED 1R0.0]
Running...
Enter an integer: K
Enter an integer: hello
Enter an integer: 8.794
The integer you input was: 8
```

While this number is not an integer, the system is able to construct an integer from a decimal by ignoring the decimal point and the digits to the right. This entry is accepted, and the value 8 is assigned to the input variable.

The list of "Enter an integer:" prompt statements can make a program unsightly. This can be cleaned up somewhat by having the program clear the screen before repeating the prompt. A simple way to accomplish this is with the PAGE(OUTPUT) procedure.

12. Add the PAGE procedure as shown:

```
PROGRAM GRACEFUL;

VAR I,ERROR_CODE : INTEGER;

BEGIN
    {$I-}
    REPEAT
        PAGE(OUTPUT);
        WRITE('Enter an integer: ');
        READ(I);
        ERROR_CODE:=IORESULT;
        READLN;
    UNTIL ERROR_CODE=0;
    {$I+}
    WRITELN('The integer you input was: ',I);
END.
```

13. Run the program.

```
Enter an integer: _
```

If you were watching closely, you saw the legend "Running..." flash briefly on the screen before the PAGE function cleared it.

14. Type **five** and press **Enter**.

```
Enter an integer: _
```

The program ignores your attempt to supply invalid input, clears the screen, and requests the input again. This is a more professional screen presentation than simply letting error messages accumulate.

15. Check several more invalid input values to verify the performance of the program.

16. Enter a valid INTEGER to end the program.

WHAT YOU HAVE LEARNED

- REPEAT loops
- IORESULT

REVIEW

1. What is IORESULT?

2. What advantage is there to using IORESULT to check for input errors?

3. What is the minimum number of times a REPEAT loop is executed?

4. What is the maximum number of times a REPEAT loop is executed?

5. What is the function of the {$I–} and {$I+} compiler directives?

6. What kind of expression is used to terminate a REPEAT loop?

7. What command will clear the screen?

Module 29
WHILE LOOPS

KEY TOPICS

- WHILE DO loops
- Avoiding infinite loops

PRACTICE SESSION

The WHILE loop is similar to the REPEAT loop. The difference is that the REPEAT loop is always executed at least once.

PREPARATION Use the G(et command in the Filer to make PAYROLL the current workfile. Enter the Editor.

```
>Edit: A(djust C(opy D(el F(ind I(nsert J(ump K(ol M(argin P(age ? [ED 1R0.0]
PROGRAM PAYROLL;

VAR HOURS, CLAMS: INTEGER;

BEGIN
    WRITE('How many hours were worked? ');
    READLN(HOURS);
    IF (HOURS < 0) OR (HOURS > 168) THEN
        WRITELN('The number of hours is invalid.')
    ELSE
    BEGIN
        IF HOURS <= 40 THEN
            CLAMS := HOURS * 6
        ELSE
            CLAMS := 40 * 6 + (HOURS-40) * 9;
        WRITE('Pay this harvester ',CLAMS,' clams.');
    END
END.
```

LEARNING ACTIVITY The "test" portion of a REPEAT loop is located at the bottom of the loop. As a result, the code in the loop is always executed at least once. There are times when you do not necessarily want a loop executed at all. The WHILE loop performs the same function as the REPEAT loop, except that the "test" is at the top of the loop.

Simple WHILE Loop The PAYROLL program you developed has a fundamental limitation in that it must be R(un for each worker. What is needed is a technique to compute the pay for all the workers.

Many businesses add and drop employees each week. A FOR loop would require that you count the number of employees each time you ran the program.

Pascal provides an end-of-file function, EOF, which is set every time an input operation is processed. On the keyboard, EOF can be set to TRUE when entering the final value in a list of input data by pressing **Ctrl-C** instead of **Enter**.

The structure of the PAYROLL program is already complex. Therefore, instead of making the program more complex by making the existing code a BEGIN END group within a loop, first make the existing code a procedure called CALCULATE.

1. Declare PROCEDURE CALCULATE containing all of the existing code. You need to change the ending "." to ";".

```
>Edit: A(djust C(opy D(el F(ind I(nsert J(ump K(ol M(argin P(age ? [ED 1R0.0]
PROGRAM PAYROLL;

PROCEDURE CALCULATE;

VAR HOURS, CLAMS: INTEGER;

BEGIN
    WRITE('How many hours were worked? ');
    READLN(HOURS);
    IF (HOURS < 0) OR (HOURS > 168) THEN
        WRITELN('The number of hours is invalid.')
    ELSE
    BEGIN
        IF HOURS <= 40 THEN
            CLAMS := HOURS * 6
        ELSE
            CLAMS := 40 * 6 + (HOURS-40) * 9;
        WRITE('Pay this harvester ',CLAMS,' clams.');
    END
END;
```

Notice that the PROCEDURE statement is placed above the VAR statement. The effect of this is to make the variables HOURS and CLAMS "local" to the procedure.

2. Add a main program segment after the procedures as follows:

```
BEGIN
    WHILE NOT EOF(INPUT) DO CALCULATE;
END.
```

3. Run the program.

4. Specify 25 hours.

```
Running...
How many hours were worked? 25
Pay this harvester 150 clams.How many hours were worked? _
```

The program has provided the correct answer and has looped back to ask for the next harvester's hours. You can already see some formatting problems.

5. Type **10** and press **Ctrl-C**.

```
Command: E(dit, R(un, F(ile, C(omp, X(ecute, U(ser restart [ED 1R0.0]
Running...
How many hours were worked? 25
Pay this harvester 150 clams.How many hours were worked? 10
Pay this harvester 60 clams.
```

Compound WHILE Loop The screen becomes cluttered quickly. One way to clear the screen is through the use of the PAGE function. The statement PAGE(OUTPUT) clears the screen.

1. Modify the main program body as shown:

```
BEGIN
    WHILE NOT EOF(INPUT) DO
    BEGIN
        PAGE(OUTPUT);
        CALCULATE
    END;
END.
```

2. Run the program. Type **25** and press **Enter**.

```
How many hours were worked? _
```

If you were watching closely, you saw the legend "Running . . ." flash briefly on the screen before the PAGE procedure cleared it.

3. Type **10** and press **Ctrl-C** to end the program.

It is necessary to insert additional statements to cause the program to wait before going on.

4. Modify the main program to read:

```
BEGIN
    WHILE NOT EOF(INPUT) DO
    BEGIN
        PAGE(OUTPUT);
        CALCULATE;
        WRITELN;
        WRITELN('Press ENTER to continue, Ctrl-C to end.');
        READLN
    END;
END.
```

This modification has made two changes at once. First, the display will stay on the screen until the user provides an input. Second, all data is now input with the **Enter** key. The last READLN statement is the one which will set the EOF function immediately prior to its test.

5. Run the program.

6. Try a variety of numbers as input.

7. Terminate the program by pressing **Ctrl-C**.

The WHILE loop allows you to repeat a series of statements until a condition is satisfied.

Infinite Loops Beginning programmers often forget to assure that a loop will actually end.

1. Clear the workfile and create the following program:

```
PROGRAM FOREVER;

BEGIN
    WHILE 1=1 DO
        WRITELN('This program will run forever if not stopped.');
END.
```

2. Run the program.

```
This program will run forever if not stopped.
This program will run forever if not stopped.
This program will run forever if not stopped.
This program will run forever if not stopped.
This program will run forever if not stopped.
This program will run forever if not stopped.
This program will run forever if not stopped.
This program will run forever if not stopped.
This program will run forever if not stopped.
This program will run forever if not stopped.
This program will run forever if not stopped.
This program will run forever if not stopped.
This program will run forever if not stopped.
This program will run forever if not stopped.
This program will run forever if not stopped.
This program will run forever if not stopped.
This program will run forever if not stopped.
This program will run forever if not stopped.
This program will run forever if not stopped.
This program will run forever if not stopped.
This program will run forever if not stopped.
This program will run forever if not stopped.
This program will run forever if not stopped.
This program will run forever if not stopped.
This program will run forever if not stopped.
This program will run forever if not stopped.
This program will run forever if not stopped.
This program will run forever if not stopped.
```

The **Break** key is the upper right key on the keyboard. The word "Break" is printed on the front of the key instead of the top. (Press **Fn-B** on the IBM PCjr.)

3. Press **Ctrl-Break** to end the program.

4. Press the **Spacebar** to re-initialize the system.

5. Start the Editor. Modify the program as follows:

```
PROGRAM FOREVER;

VAR THE_END_OF_TIME : BOOLEAN;

BEGIN
    THE_END_OF_TIME:=FALSE;
    REPEAT
        WRITELN('This program will run till the end of time.')
    UNTIL THE_END_OF_TIME;
END.
BEGIN
    WHILE NOT EOF(INPUT) DO CALCULATE;
END.
```

6. Run the program.

```
This program will run till the end of time.
This program will run till the end of time.
This program will run till the end of time.
This program will run till the end of time.
This program will run till the end of time.
This program will run till the end of time.
This program will run till the end of time.
This program will run till the end of time.
This program will run till the end of time.
This program will run till the end of time.
This program will run till the end of time.
This program will run till the end of time.
This program will run till the end of time.
This program will run till the end of time.
This program will run till the end of time.
This program will run till the end of time.
This program will run till the end of time.
This program will run till the end of time.
This program will run till the end of time.
This program will run till the end of time.
This program will run till the end of time.
This program will run till the end of time.
This program will run till the end of time.
This program will run till the end of time.
This program will run till the end of time.
```

7. Press **Ctrl-Break** to end the program.

8. Press the **Spacebar** to re-initialize the system.

Writing programs that must be stopped by pressing **Ctrl -Break** is exceptionally poor programming style. The examples here are straightforward enough for you to immediately see that they will never end normally.

When you write a program loop, make certain that statements inside the scope of the loop will change the loop condition so that the loop will eventually terminate normally. Keeping loops short through the use of procedures and careful indentation of program steps will make it easier to verify the correctness of the programs you write.

WHAT YOU HAVE LEARNED

- WHILE DO loops
- Avoiding infinite loops
- Programming is hard work

REVIEW

1. What does EOF mean?

2. How can EOF be used in a program?

3. What is the advantage of a compound WHILE loop over a simple WHILE loop?

4. How do you avoid an infinite loop?

5. What is the minimum number of times a WHILE loop is executed?

6. How can you set EOF to TRUE when using keyboard input?

APPENDIX A
RESERVED WORDS AND PREDECLARED IDENTIFIERS

The lists of reserved words and predeclared identifiers include Pascal features not discussed in this volume. They are included to assist you in developing variable and constant names.

RESERVED WORDS

AND
ARRAY
BEGIN
CASE
CONST
DIV
DO
DOWNTO
ELSE
END
EXTERNAL
FILE
FOR
FUNCTION
GOTO
IF
IMPLEMENTATION
IN
INTERFACE
LABEL
MOD
NOT
OF
OR
PACKED
PROCEDURE
PROCESS
PROGRAM
RECORD
REPEAT
SEGMENT
SET
THEN
TO
TYPE
UNIT
UNTIL
USES
VAR
WHILE
WITH

PREDECLARED IDENTIFIERS

ABS
ARCTAN
ATAN
ATTACH
BLOCKREAD
BOOLEAN
CHAR
CHR
CLOSE
CONCAT
COPY
COS
DELETE
DISPOSE
EOF
EOLN
EXIT
EXP
FALSE
FILLCHAR
GET
GOTOXY
HALT
IDSEARCH
INPUT
INSERT
INTEGER
INTERACTIVE
IORESULT
KEYBOARD
LENGTH
LN
LOG

MARK
MAXINT
MEMAVAIL
MEMLOCK
MEMSWAP
MOVELEFT
MOVERIGHT
NEW
NIL
ODD
ORD
OUTPUT
PAGE
PMACHINE
POS
PRED
PROCESSID
PUT
PWROFTEN
READ
READLN
REAL
RELEASE
REWRITE
ROUND
SCAN
SEEK
SEMAPHORE
SEMINIT
SIGNAL
SIN
SIZEOF
SQR
SQRT
START
STR
STRING
SUCC
TEXT
TIME
TREESEARCH
TRUE
TRUNC
UNITBUSY
UNITCLEAR
UNITREAD
UNITSTATUS
UNITWAIT
UNITWRITE
VARAVAIL
VARDISPOSE
VARNEW
WRITE
WRITELN

APPENDIX B
PASCAL SYNTAX

The specification of the language has been abbreviated for clarity to include only those Pascal features discussed in this volume.

Notation:

[Anything in square brackets is optional.]

{Anything in curly brackets can be repeated any number of times.}

```
program =
        PROGRAM program-name ;
        [USES unitname]
        [constant-declaration]
        [variable-declaration]
        [function-declarations and/or procedure-declarations]
        BEGIN
                statement {;
                statement}
        END.

procedure =
        PROCEDURE procedure-name ;
        [constant-declaration]
        [variable-declaration]
        BEGIN
                statement {;
                statement}
        END;

function =
        FUNCTION function-name
        [(variable-name {,variable-name} :
        type-name
        {;variable-name {,variable-name}
        : type-name})] :
        type-name;
```

```
        [constant-declaration]
        [variable-declaration]
        BEGIN
                statement {;
                statement}
        END;

constant-declaration =
        CONST constant-name = constant;
                {constant-name = constant;}

variable-declaration =
        VAR variable-name {,variable-name}: type-name;
                {variable-name {,identifier}: type-name;}

type-name =
        INTEGER
        REAL
        CHAR
        STRING

assignment statement =
        variable-name := expression

case-statement =
        CASE expression OF
                constant-list : statement
                {; constant-list : statement}
                [;]
        END

compound-statement =
        BEGIN
                statement
                {; statement}
        END

for-to-statement =
        FOR variable := start-value
                TO end-value
                DO statement
```

for-downto-statement =
  FOR variable **:=** start-value
    DOWNTO end-value
    DO statement

if-statement =
  IF Boolean-expression **THEN**
    statement
  [**ELSE**
    statement]

page-statement =
  PAGE(OUTPUT)

read-statement =
  READ([variable-name {, variable-name}**)**

readln-statement =
  READLN[**(**variable-name {,variable-name}**)**]

repeat-statement =
  REPEAT
    statement {;
    statement}
  UNTIL Boolean-expression

while-statement =
  WHILE Boolean-expression **DO**
    statement

write-statement =
  WRITE (output-item {, output-item}**)**

writeln-statement =
  WRITELN [**(**output-item {, output-item}**)**]

APPENDIX C
EXECUTION ERRORS

0 Fatal system error
1 Invalid index, value out of range
2 No segment, bad code file
3 Procedure not present at exit time
4 Stack overflow
5 Integer overflow
6 Divide by zero
7 Invalid memory reference <bus timed out>
8 User break
9 Fatal system I/O error
10 User I/O error
11 Unimplemented instruction
12 Floating point math error
13 String too long
14 Halt, Break Point
15 Bad Block
16 Break Point
17 Incompatible Real Number Size
18 Set Too Large
19 Segment Too Large

All run-time errors cause the system to I(nitialize itself; FATAL errors cause the system to rebootstrap. Some FATAL errors leave the system in an irreparable state, in which case you must rebootstrap.

INDEX